Higher Education in Europe and the United States of America

A Diverse Collection of Essays

Henry Wasser
with Solidelle Fortier

UNIVERSITY PRESS OF AMERICA,® INC.
Lanham • Boulder • New York • Toronto • Plymouth, UK

Copyright © 2007 by
University Press of America,® Inc.
4501 Forbes Boulevard
Suite 200
Lanham, Maryland 20706
UPA Acquisitions Department (301) 459-3366

PO Box 317
Oxford
OX2 9RU, UK

Library of Congress Control Number: 2007928245
ISBN-13: 978-0-7618-3778-7 (clothbound : alk. paper)
ISBN-10: 0-7618-3778-7 (clothbound : alk. paper)
ISBN-13: 978-0-7618-3779-4 (paperback : alk. paper)
ISBN-10: 0-7618-3779-5 (paperback : alk. paper)

∞™ The paper used in this publication meets the minimum
requirements of American National Standard for Information
Sciences—Permanence of Paper for Printed Library Materials,
ANSI Z39.48—1984

To the memory of Chancellor Joseph Murphy who appointed me Research Scholar of Comparative Higher Education after my service as chair of the City University of New York Faculty Senate, an assignment that led to much of the research and analysis culminating in these articles.

Contents

Preface

These essays constitute an exploration into several aspects of what may be called the culture of university policy and change and inter-disciplinarity. They deal with comparative analysis, the role of intellectuals, the corporatization of universities, a case study of a post-secondary institution and economic development, blurring of financial and structural boundaries between public and private higher education, legitimacy, crisis and reform in university trustees. They were presented in Leyden, Maastricht and Enschede, The Netherlands, Antwerp, Belgium, Porto, Portugal, Dijon and Marseilles, France, Vancouver, Canada, Warwick, England, and Ankara, Turkey, at conferences sponsored and organized by the International Association of American Studies, World Congress of Comparative Education, Consortium for Higher Education Researchers, European Association for Institutional Research, Canadian Association for Higher Education, International Conference on Higher Education, American-Scandinavian Society, and Massachusetts Historical Society.

The period of time covered is roughly the last decade, and the most recent development is the movement toward privatization. As Robert H. C. Adams has written, privatization is an area in which the United States leads and in which universities are competitive in focusing and maintaining the level of excellence of elite universities. The assumption is that fewer successful competitors will result, and the prevailing value system insures that less attention is given to assuring common, minimal standards of quality or of opportunity applying to all members of universities, rather than to the standards of the best institutions, in contrast to European universities.

These often-comparative studies may be viewed as forays into what might generally be seen as American Studies — seen comparatively — with reference to higher education policy, sociology, literature and economics.

Introduction

The present state of universities, or more broadly higher education, is one of flux, in a period of radical change. This collection of papers presented over a number of years at international conferences are short encounters with key issues. The subjects covered are numerous, if not comprehensive. Funding, autonomy, government intervention, corporatization, short cycle, legitimacy, economic impact, role of trustees, relation to industry, research, diversity, curricular reform and comparative methodology are discussed and analyzed briefly. This list does not differ greatly from the significant areas in higher education Ladislav Cyerch cited in 1992 for reference in the future—these being curriculum, global and diversified systems, institutional autonomy, responsibility and responsiveness, competitiveness, equality of opportunity, continuing education, cooperation with industry, use of communication and information technologies, contribution to economic and social cohesion and to regional development, and foreign language teaching and learning. Currently, such topics as marketing, commercializing, managerializing the university are forefronted. Conditions for teaching have been sharply altered by the employment of adjuncts and part-timers that perform more than 50% of all higher-education instruction.

Yet Richard Rorty reminds us that the role of higher education, unlike that provided in schools, is no longer to incorporate given truths but to stimulate the imagination and the critical mind, to fuel doubts about unquestioned truths and the consensus of predominant prejudices. And Jean-Jacques Paul argues that universities have been built upon different layers of sedimented knowledge, upon partial adaptations to successive environmental changes. They have to preserve functions such as promoting general and theoretical knowledge and encouraging reflection and critical thinking. Clark Kerr warns us that in American higher education, changes influenced by the market are accepted in a way that reforms originating in concerns for educational policy are not.—in Kerr's striking wording, an appropriate emblem for the American colleges might be the traditional open book but lying on a sales counter.

Of course, there have always been hostages to fortune. Kogan and Henkel point out that appointments are made in deference to areas likely to be favored in the marketplace of sponsorship rather than by strict ordering of academic merits of applicants. Merging of academic work with practice and the pursuit of knowledge for its own sake with market demands, may affect the standards of the academic enterprise. New material may force more traditional subjects aside. With all these changes, governance, as Donald Kennedy declares,—the organizational context that directs how choices are made and who makes them—is absolutely critical.

Stephen Stigler insists that faculty own the university and competition among and within universities is a competition among faculties. Even if actual ownership is constrained by rules imposed by trustees and vested in academic administrators who may serve at the pleasure of faculty, in fact if not in name, faculty act as if they own their own universities. While Stigler's views may seem irrelevant in this dominant age of privatization and comprehensive power of increasing managerialism in universities, they are nevertheless a striking reminder of what has been lost and might be regained. Past institutional dependence on the scholar-administrator and action conditioned on faculty's perception of the university's specific intellectual goals has given way to the professional manager and administrator. Long discussions among faculty to provide stable environment for exploration into unknown intellectual territory has declined in the face of administrator-directed focus groups. Programs are determined by congressional earmarking of funds for projects without any review. Agencies steer their own priorities in the setting of research agendas. Intellectual competition, Stigler maintains, is fundamental to faculty success, and whatever diminishes that competition diminishes those institutions. Moves toward a greater degree of specialization must be guided by faculty who can make the most informed judgment of disciplinary strength.

Current emphasis on marketing, commercializing, managerializing the university have darkened the picture painted by Stigler. Conditions of teaching have been altered by the fact that at least 50% of university instruction is done by part-timers, graduate assistants and adjuncts. Industry has assumed a far greater role in funding and determining the conditions and content of research over recent years.

A recently published compendium (2005 revision of 1999 book) by Altbach et al., in dealing with leadership, accountability, access, finance, technology, academic freedom, the canon, governance and race, does not confront the overarching problems in this Age of Privatization of marketing, professional managerializing, blurred boundaries between public and private higher education, the metamorphosis of a public into a private good. This sea-change in university or higher-education policy and activity is best described as occurring in an age of privatization, an epoch of corporatization, metamorphosis of a public good into a private good, and characterized in books with titles like universities in crisis, universities in ruins, universities inc., academic strategy, the managerial revolution in American higher education, the privatization of higher education, and academic capitalism.

Probably the age of privatization, a phrase used by Roger Geiger and others, best characterizes current dynamics in higher education.

Privatization, as many have noted, is deeply rooted in United States history and culture. Levels of direct support from state legislatures progressively decline at many of the major state universities, in some cases to substantially less than 20% of their annual budgets, which must be made up by private funds—donor, tuition increases, etc. But as Robert McAdams declares, privatization is not exclusively a matter of structural autonomy and formal freedom of action. It is closely coupled with more subtle transformations in perceptions, assumptions and values. What was once commonly thought of as new knowledge, for example, is increasingly characterized as "intellectual property." The same can be applied to the growing entrepreneurialism that can be documented in university planning, cost-accounting, "out-sourcing," auxiliary enterprises, outside constructing for ancillary operations and exploitation of faculty patents in pursuit of profit (often shared with the inventor, using various formulae) as well as public benefits. Inevitably, this results in the broadening of faculty oversight.

The public-private interface shifts toward the private directions. Closure of major corporate labs widens the shift of industrial research to short-term rather than basic problems and consequently impacting university research. Great variety of university-affiliated activities leads some universities to concentrate on applied forms of research, permitting faculty to be funded for long-term activities outside the normal scope of academic programs in university-industry research centers. Fear does arise that through consultancy the interaction between academics and business might lead to "back door" leakage of university research as industrialists wander unchecked around labs. Moreover, academics might be distracted from their core research and teaching to research linkage. Institution's insurers might be alarmed by the prospect of vicarious liability from advice given on work undertaken through consulting.

Roger Geiger, writing extensively on the issue, is judicious and often neutral in his assessments as we enter the age of privatization. He characterizes the American university as displaying and responding to signposts on the path to privatization, declaring that universities behave more and more like intelligent firms than benighted bureaucracies.

He, along with other analysts, has noted that financial stringency has given administrators increased leverage to affect a new managerial style, which inhibits faculty governance power. Privatization also shifts the cost of higher education to students and parents (increased tuition fees beyond the consumer price index for inflation), even though universities were receiving large returns from patents and faculty-linked firms in such areas as biotechnology.

Engaged in patenting and venture capital, universities were also involved in investing, transacting business and administering ancillary activities, pursuit of gifts, and holders of large endowments. Consequently, universities became sophisticated investors, resorting to asset allocation models, professional money managers, program trading and other Wall Street stratagems. They were also engaged entrepreneurially in the running of campus, auxiliary enterprises, outsourcing to private corporations—bookstores, food service, dormitories, marketing, logos, trademarks of sportswear companies, brand names, beverages, and junk food companies.

The "managerial revolution" in higher education has weakened, if not narrowed, the sphere in which traditional decision-making occurred. Administrators direct their energy to strategic planning, cost-centered budgeting and tactics derived from business-sector managerialism, such as Total Quality Management, which even came into academic departments.

In retrospect, it appears that federal government's large funding of higher education put purchasing power in the hands of students rather than public institutions and thus rejuvenated private universities. Moreover, leading private institutions have greater control over their income stream than public universities. Most conspicuous is taxpayer money given each year to private universities in the State of New York for each bachelor's, master's, and doctor's degrees produced with few restrictions as to the expenditure of that money, often spent on research, celebrity appointments, decreasing teaching loads, and student financial aid and services. Public universities do, however, have an advantage where a large base of operations is necessary to accommodate a larger scale and scope of knowledge-based activities, which may permit more ready adaptation to future research-based technologies. For both public and private universities, however, commercialization of their research is both a service to the public and a source of institutional revenue.

As universities expand their peripheral activities, immobilizing their academic core, they import professional managers and make their managerial culture more like that of the market in which they compete. These developments lead policy analysts to wonder at what point does this loosely coupled adaptive system cease to be a university.

Anthony Smith, citing dominant instrumentality, asserts that the university has lost its position as the center of authoritative knowledge, displaced by think tanks, private corporations and media companies. Knowledge has been ousted from its priority in the pursuit of "transferable" skills, competencies without content, alongside widely marketable "analytic abilities, "problem solving" and "communication skills." Meanwhile, the university (alma mater) has become a brand, students have become consumers, teacher's work on contracts (and talk of "product"), and the corporate presence is everywhere, together with the corporate mindset. Performativity has triumphed. Entrepreneurship is pervasive. Managerial and "audit" cultures are present, and universities have responded with mission statements and business plans.

There are some exceptions to the domination of professional managerialism in universities. In Norway, for example, after extensive interviews, analysts conclude that non-academic administrators have not expanded their control over academic matters in universities. Administrators see themselves as "serving" faculty, where their American equivalents often view themselves as leading faculty in process and in change. They believe themselves to be reactive rather than active and respect faculty supremacy in governance.

But even in Scandinavian universities there is a felt need for more pro-active managerial leadership and consequently the formation of training, mainly as "tool-box" courses. Collegial leadership remains a necessary prerequisite for a change process characterized by renewal and continuity. In this pattern, academic leadership needs to be understood as a collective process and as an individual characteristic, social construction is negotiated, and forms of consensus-building necessary for quality improvement are developed.

The Goretzka-Larsen study finds additional sharp contrasts between U.S. and Norway in their comparative study of higher education. Where American administrators lead faculty actively, Norwegians serve faculty reactively. The clear chasm in Norway between role of administrator and that of academic leader is blurred in the U.S.A. Organizational development is the responsibility of elected bodies of governance and academic leaders in Norway and of administrators in the U.S.A. The primary "production work" does not involve administrators heavily as in the U.S.A. The "agents of change" thus in Norway are faculty and their leaders, and in the U.S.A. administrators and managers. Universities continue to become renowned for the quality of their teaching, research and scholarship, not for their efficient administration. Still, universally it can be concluded that while the vestiges of the traditional system of university governance and management may remain in place—with privileged position given the academic community in decision-making and leadership, their real influence on how the university evolves has eroded and that of a more professionalized and permanent management stratum has increased.

A recent survey by the Federal Education Department in Australia has reached a conclusion matched by many Western nations. Academia has been altered by the "great growth in communications and information technology," by a strong change in management styles from the collegial to the managerial, by greatly increased use of casual staff and by a decline in the relative status, salaries, prestige and general attractiveness of employment as an academic.

However, a recent account by Jürgen Enders, Barbara Kehm, and Uwe Schimank tells a somewhat different story for Germany. It utilizes Clark's four mechanisms for international comparisons of higher education systems: political guidance of universities by state authorities; the self-regulation of oligarchic academic communities; competition between and within universities for strategic resources and for customers of their services; and hierarchical self-guidance of universities by their leaders. In category one the study characterizes the German university system as a combination of nourishment and control by the state and the state's constitutional duty to respect the "freedom of teaching and research." Secondly, academic self-regulation is strongly oligarchic, chair-holders being the dominant decision makers with other professors and academic staff, non-academic employees and students clearly in subordinate positions. In the matter of competition for resources and customers, Germany lacks the American combination of high competitive pressure and strong university leadership. Finally, as to hierarchical organizational self-governance, Germany contrasts with the "professionalization" of university leadership and power centers in the U.S.A. In this age of privatization and corporatization, the German experience seems "odd-man-out."

The dominant American experience seems captured in the title of a recent book, *The American University: Mission Centered and Market Smart*, and in the assertions of advocates that higher education is really another well-run industry where the most successful enterprises have learned to bring to market programs that will attract customers and sponsors. American "boosterism" differs markedly from the still extant, only moderately changed European university traditions (Robert Zemsky and others, Rutgers University Press, 2005). These "boosters" want university leaders to be market-smart managers prepared to spend personal and institutional capital in pursuit of public purpose, which they do not define.

The papers in this collection were written in a period of time in which decisive issues in higher education moved from the comprehensive, multi-varsity university to blurred distinctions between public and private higher education, in a period in which the function of the state with respect to universities changed sharply, a period in which feminist, Afro-American, diversity, gay/lesbian issues came to be more clearly defined in universities, a period in which celebrity status and C.E.O. salaries were achieved in academia, a period in which instrumentalism and professionalism came to overshadow traditional knowledge values in the university, a period in which market values came to fruition. These essays reflect, if only glancingly, these dynamics within higher education in the last decade. Some years ago, Bjørn Wittrock wondered who would greet the morning sun "after the darkest hour" for universities, whether the resuscitated scholarly communities of Peter Scott or the academic tribes of Tony Becher or the "dinosaurs" of Harold Perkin. No matter what, he was optimistic that rigorous analysis would influence development.

Yet beyond Wittrock's optimism lay the heavy weight of the commodification and corporatization of the university. Analysis, contrary to his wish, did not effectively clarify or influence development and has become even less significant in this age of privatization. What follows may in a minor way reflect this.

Chapter One

The Role of the Public University Trustee: City University of New York: A Case History

Henry Wasser

CUNY's Board of Trustees fits the standard definition of a state-wide governing lay board in so far as it has final responsibility for budget development, resource allocation, and approval of academic programs and appointment of campus and system chief executives. It differs from many boards in that its jurisdiction includes two-year community colleges, four-year technical college, senior liberal arts colleges, medical school programs, law school, graduate school for doctoral programs, school of social work, school of professional studies, school of journalism, and a college of criminal justice. Many states have boards for each of the three kinds of college structures. Some have advisory boards for each college within the system but CUNY does not.

As do most governing boards, CUNY functions as an advocate for institutions under its jurisdiction and tries to buffer these institutions from external political forces while at the same time holding them accountable for meeting the public needs. It attempts to adapt the objectives of the university system to the needs of the state. There are, of course, constraints. The Governor appoints ten members, the Mayor of New York City selects five members; the Chairman of the University Faculty Senate and Chairman of the University Student Senate are ex officio. The faculty representative has a vote on all operating committees of the Board but not on the Board itself, while the student representative by act of the legislature has a vote on the board and all operating committees.

Since the lay board members are political appointees, they are often subject to strong pressures from the governor and to a lesser degree from the mayor. And, of course, the faculty and student heads are constantly subject to the influence of the majority within their constituency.

1

The quality of Board members has varied. When CUNY belonged completely to the City of New York, the Mayors appointed a screening committee of prominent public and academic figures to nominate a list of qualified candidates from whom the Mayor made his selection. The present system in operation since 1979 when the State of New York took over most of the financing of CUNY at the request of the City when it faced bankruptcy does not provide for a screening committee.

The composition of the Board of Trustees customarily reflects the ethnic and social constituencies of the city, as is to be expected in a public institution. One recent board had the following representation:

Ethnic / racial diversity:
    6 Jewish American
    4 Black
    3 Italian American
    2 Hispanic (Puerto Rican)
    1 Irish American
    1 Chinese American
Occupation:*
    5 lawyers
    4 former government officials (elected an appointed)
    3 investment counselors / bankers
    3 academics
    1 businessman
    1 school administrator
    1 student
*some members are in two categories
    By gender:
    9 men
    8 women
    Miscellaneous information:
    2 Multi-millionaires
    2 Primarily union officials
    2 Primarily politicians
    3 Primarily academics

It must be noted that all the trustees are active in community affairs, especially those involving their own ethnic or racial group—indeed such activity and influence are the basic reason for their selection.

The Board has made the customary separation of concerns—it deals with policy along the role of advocacy and conservation, leaving management to the appointed system and college heads. Members do not always find it possible to differentiate clearly between policy and administration, leading at times to accusations of board intrusion by chancellor / presidents and executive intervention in board prerogatives. No executive, however, questions the board's dominant role in presidential appointment, retention and evaluation. Faculty and students may be uneasy about this control—all search committees are chaired by a trustee and while students and faculty are represented, all actions must have a majority of trustees on the committee approving.

Case histories are perhaps the most accurate way of revealing the reality of board operation.

1. Some years ago, a sharp conflict over authority broke out between the System Chancellor and the Trustees' Chairman. Mutual accusations of jurisdictional interference were made. The Chancellor submitted his resignation but continued the struggle, and the Governor was finally persuaded to uphold the Chancellor, not the Chairman of the Board whose term of office was not renewed by the Governor.

2. As a municipal institution, CUNY, particularly in its prior existence as separate colleges had been tuition free. The increasing economic difficulties brought a strong political group to the demand for institution of tuition. Such action is the responsibility of the Trustees. The Board Chairman and a majority of trustees opposed instituting tuition. The Mayor and Chancellor favored such. The outcome was that the Chairman lost the battle and resigned along with other trustee advocates of free tuition. They were then replaced by the Mayor with appointees who proceeded to vote for tuition.

3. Although CUNY already had an association with a leading medical school, strong political, community groups in the borough of Queens pressed for CUNY's establishing a medical school there. Arguments were presented—*for*—the medical school would emphasize public, primary-care medicine particularly for ghetto, minority areas—*against*—medical schools were already producing too many doctors and financing a medical school would drain necessary budget from all other units of the university. The initiative was political, the reluctant trustees finally approved when it became clear that the Governor (from that background) favored establishment of the Medical School. The struggle is not yet over, since, the medical program relies on association with other medical schools.

4. One of the Board's stated functions is to approve a general grading policy. The wording of that responsibility in the By-laws is ambiguous. The trustees have not approved, at the initiative of administrators, a policy removing a failing grade (F) from a transcript of a student who has taken and passed a course the second time. Thus, the time-honored policy of all earned

grades being recorded in transcript is to be changed. The faculty is strongly opposed to what it considers a violation of its prerogatives (curriculum, grading, etc.). The struggle continues.

Public hearings, by law, must be held by the Board of Trustees on all items in a forthcoming agenda to be voted on in public meeting. At such public hearings all who ask may speak for three minutes. A hotly debated issue may have as many as sixty or seventy speakers. Trustees are supposed to be in attendance at such hearing, but on average no more than six or seven will be present. Occasionally, however, a public hearing may postpone or even modify an action.

For CUNY, all voting by trustees must be at public meetings, except personnel actions, which are taken in executive session (or private meetings).

5. A chancellor wished a president to retire earlier than the president intended. The president refused. The dispute became public. Both took their case to the trustees who in this matter did not completely support its chief executive. He resigned. The president will retire one year later than the chancellor wished him to. As a result of this imbroglio, the Board of Trustees has approved a new policy defining a limit on the terms of current presidents and setting the terms of new presidential appointments (also chancellor) in place of the current indefinite appointments. Before final action, however, the process involves consultation with the executive committee of the university student senate by an ad hoc committee of trustees appointed by the chairperson of the board, as well as a public hearing where anyone may speak briefly to the point-item of the agenda before final vote by the full board at a stated public meeting.

A mere list of details of the Board's jurisdiction reveals possible confusion in distinguishing between policy and management:

sets fees and tuition structure
submits request budget
approves allocation of final budget
approves routinely all appointments—faculty and non-faculty
actively involved in selection of chancellor, presidents, vice-chancellors
approves new programs, eliminates old programs
approves creation, elimination and merger of departments
approves general grading policy
approves constitution / governance of individual colleges, students, faculty
    councils as well as those of university-wide faculty and student senates
approves of collective bargaining (union) contracts
hears appeals of dismissed staff

The trustees operate as a committee of the whole without an executive committee but with six standing committees—Budget, Facilities, Student Affairs, Academic Affairs, Faculty/Staff/Administration Personnel and Long-Range Planning.

In practice, however, the Board of Trustees generally accepts the recommendations in these matters of the Chancellor and his headquarters staff. Occasionally, central staff recommendations are modified, even reversed, on the basis of additional discussion and analysis by trustees including faculty and student ones and an absolute majority vote of the board.

In addition to the required public hearing on the agenda items for Board meetings (ten a year), the law requires the trustees once a year to hold a public hearing in each of New York City's five boroughs—Queens, Manhattan, Brooklyn, Bronx and Staten Island—where community representatives or indeed individuals may speak briefly (three minutes) on any topic that seems somehow relevant to the operation of public higher education in the city e.g. day care, community use of university buildings, university participation in community activities (anti-smoking, anti-pollution, traffic, crime in the area of the college, courses for the elderly, re-establishing free tuition, celebration of human rights, policy on Aids, etc.).

There are, moreover, a number of apparent contradictions with respect to the trustees.

Faculty retired at the age of seventy, at least before 1994 when university exemption from general law was removed, but there has never been a stipulation for trustees of CUNY, although the governing board of the State University of New York has an age limit of seventy-five.

The State legislature of New York in response to several financial corruption scandals among its members passed a financial disclosure act, which it then proceeded to have applicable to all state agencies and staff. The lay board a CUNY, along with other lay boards, unsalaried, balked at disclosing their finances; several threatened to resign. The law was finally modified to permit lay boards to devise their own mode of financial disclosure, although at present the original requirement remains for academic staff.

In addition to apparent contradictions, there are constraints exercised by state executive. Trustees cannot shift moneys from capital to operating budget, no matter the necessity they may see for such change in crisis. It can, however, approve shifting of funds from OTPS (other than personnel services) to PS (personnel services) or vice-versa in the interest of budget rationality.

Trustees also believe they have an obligation to lobby for their requested budget with the legislature and the executive in the capital of the State of New

York. Once a year they travel to Albany for two-day stays to talk with members of the Assembly, the Senate, the Governor's staff about CUNY's proposed budget, specifically certain key items they particularly want to see approved. They may see the leader of the Assembly, the leader of the Senate and occasionally the Governor.

Additional case histories help round out the account:

6. CUNY, along with much of the nation, was dissatisfied with the education of schoolteachers. On the initiative of a trustee, a former school teacher, the Board created a task force mainly of trustees and administrators, a few faculty and students which recommended more content, fewer method courses and internship in the class rooms. Trustees intended to proceed with instituting these changes by fiat rather than through established governance structures. Faculty objected to what it considered unwarranted interference by trustees with its prerogatives concerning curriculum. A public hearing was held with over eighty speakers, principally faculty. Trustees then proceeded to modify the process so that faculty bodies at each college had to approve proposed changes. With some modifications, the changes have now been instituted.

7. Influence of faculty trustee in changing the selection of an acting president of a college in crisis to one more fitted to handle the crisis.

8. Influence of student trustee in persuading the trustees not to favor an increase of tuition despite the apparent approval by governor, legislature and university administrators. To be sure, the opposition culminated in a student strike preventing classes from being held for two days. The outcome was victory for the students who influenced the trustees not to vote a tuition increase, acquiesced in by all concerned.

Some ambiguities have persistently defied resolution. For example, the chief lawyer of the university system is also Vice-Chancellor for Legal Affairs and thus reports as one of eight vice-chancellors to the Chancellor and General Counsel to the Board of Trustees reporting to the Board's chairperson. The current Vice-chancellor for Public Affairs is also Secretary of the Board of Trustees, thus serving at the same time administrative and trustee authority. Occasional conflicts of interest have arisen where board policy and executive management are not clearly differentiated and the individual wearing both hats has the uneasy decision to make as to which one he wears at a particular time.

Annual retreats for chief administrators and trustees help to resolve conflicts informally. Formal action can, to be sure, take place only at public meetings of the governing board.

CUNY's trustees do not neglect what they believe to be their societal obligations. They duly pass resolutions banning smoking in the buildings of the university, develop a policy on Aids governing faculty, staff and students so afflicted, condemning governmental actions regarding higher education elsewhere which it believes to be censorious, as in Mainland China.

But the general policy instruments remain the organization of the system, legislation, planning, financing and influence of a non-coercive kind. The trustees of CUNY are aware of the increasing market-oriented, entrepreneurial university. The center point for them may differ from the Delphi higher education project definition for Western Europe, which says that universities should occupy the intermediate position on the scale of central planning versus market orientation. Changes in university systems are mostly projected in terms of policy instruments, and the tension is between the government's desire to regulate and control the system, centrally on the one hand and the required level of self-determination, flexibility and adaptability necessary for institutions of higher education to fulfill their role and function well, on the other.

In the U.S., and for CUNY trustees in particular, government is not national or federal but state and their center point is more toward market orientation. Lay governing boards in the U.S. system of higher education by reason of representing community constituencies are likely more sensitive to society's needs and demands in its buffer and conduit function. Theirs is non-coercive pressure rather than confrontation with government and community.

Changing circumstances, after all, precede the adjustment of policy instruments. Government control is nearly always reactive in a rapidly changing society. But in CUNY's case trustees are more likely to react to state legislature and executive reaction to a changing society especially in financing than to develop planning initiatives. The governing board's policy initiatives are prone to be internal such as:

course length
duration of study
curriculum regulations
distribution of higher education facilities
distribution of consumer entitlements to higher education
quality assessment and performance indicators
budget allocation mechanism
distribution of power regarding personnel policy

Thus any conclusion as to trustees acting as buffer, conduit, communicator, policy maker, planner, promoter requires modification and explanation. Indeed, while selections from actual wording of the June 13, 1979 law passed by the New York State Assembly and Senate and signed by the Governor do not fill in the entire picture, they do testify at least to unique and traditional features of the City University and thus of the functions of its Board of Trustees with respect to mission and operation.

The City University is of vital importance as a vehicle for the upward mobility of the disadvantaged in the city of New York.

Only the strongest commitment to the special needs of an urban constituency justifies the legislature's support of an independent and unique structure for the university. Activities at the City University campuses must be undertaken in a spirit, which recognizes and responds to the imperative need for affirmative action and the positive desire to have City University personnel reflect the diverse communities, which comprise the people of the city and state of New York. In its urban environment this commitment should be evident in all the guidelines established by the board of trustees for the university's operation, from admissions and hiring to contracting for the provision of goods, services, new construction and facilities rehabilitation.

The City University shall have the powers and privileges of colleges and shall be subject to the visitation of the regents at the university of the State of New York.

The Board of Trustees shall govern and administer the City University. The control of the educational work of the City University shall rest solely in the board of trustees, which shall govern and administer all educational units of the City University.

The term of office of each appointed trustee shall be seven years renewable solely for one additional term of seven years.

A chairperson and a vice-chairperson of the Board of Trustees shall be appointed by and serve at the pleasure of the governor.

The five trustees appointed by the mayor shall be residents of the city of New York, and shall include at least one alumnus of an individual unit in the City University.

The trustees appointed by the governor shall include at least one resident of each of the five boroughs of the city of New York and shall include at least two alumni of an educational unit in the City University, including at least one other alumnus of a community college.

At least three trustees shall attend each public hearing where testimony and statements from concerned individuals about university issues will be received.

Every four years trustees must formulate a long-range plan and recommendations re such plans for new curricula, facilities change in policies re student admissions, potential student enrollments, relation to other colleges, universities, public and private within the state (for informational purposes only), projection standards, overall expenditure projections of capital and operating costs. The purpose of the above is to provide for development of regents statewide plan for higher education—submitted to review and approval of the Board of Regents and final approval by the governor—to guide, determine the development, organization and coordination of City University—copy of report to regents, to president of senate, speaker of assembly, mayor and president of City Council. Modifications of the master plan may be presented at any time.

Plans for termination or merger of a senior college or community college are subject to the approval of the legislature.

The Board of Trustees shall establish positions, departments, divisions and faculties, fix salaries of instructional and non-instructional employees, establish and conduct courses and curricula, prescribe conditions of student admission, attendance and discharge, determine tuition and fees, grant on recommendation of faculty certificates, diplomas and degrees, provide for eligibility for sabbatical leaves of absence (full-pay, half-year, half-pay full-year stipulated).

Although we have described the formal structure for power and decision-making with respect to CUNY's Board of Trustees, the question persists for researchers as well as for all the constituencies of the university. Is there behind the formal, legal statements of authority and decision-making and informal, infra reality, a locus of power outside Senate Bill 6372 and Assembly Bill 8273? Does power for many decisions in reality belong to the central administrators?

Chapter Two

Technical and General Education: A Comparative View

Henry Wasser

The tradition in Europe is to distinguish between those following theoretical studies leading to higher education and the professions and those pursuing less "noble" tracks leading directly to the world of work at a lower status level. The tradition in the U.S.A. has been to integrate, where possible, technical and general education in one, comprehensive institution or system.

More recently, Europe, as most purely exemplified in Sweden, has moved toward integration of the technical and the general, the practical and the theoretical. The 1977 reforms in Swedish higher education aligned all undergraduate studies along five occupational sectors rather than basing them, as was previously the case, upon the traditional academic disciplines—technology, administration, economic and social work, teaching, medicine and nursing work, cultural information.

A less successful effort with a similar objective in England was to establish the single institution of a tertiary college which normally would contain all forms of post-16 education and so represent a merging rather than a bridging of upper secondary and further education or a fusion of the general and the technical.

David Reeder points out that "the question of the role of education in an industrial society is also one of cultural priorities and ultimately, perhaps, what should be recognized as culture. Those educationists resistant to socio-economic pressures take a stand on the cultural argument for the intrinsic values of education; whilst the critics of modern education claim that the cultural argument is distorted by the social esteem attached to academic studies and by the failure to recognize the validity of technical culture."

Indeed, researchers have tried to identify eight models of education activity essential for a balanced curriculum. These are literary, linguistic studies, mathematics, science, social studies, creative and aesthetic activities, physical activity and religious and moral. A report from Scotland (Mann) says these should constitute two-thirds of the time table for pupils with the rest devoted to elective, optional subjects. Another (Dunning) proposes that every student receive a certificate under the theme "assessment for all." There would be three levels of award—foundation, general and credit—with national guidelines and local assessment at the school level. It must be recognized that while pupils taking courses in accounting, economics or secretarial studies are clearly enrolled in vocational preparation courses, so are pupils taking three science courses—usually for entry to a medical program—and three language classes—often for careers involving languages.

The reports from Scotland emphasize the necessity for being careful to guard against offering courses which have too much vocational preparation of a specific nature e.g. automobile skills, office skills, catering etc. and then adding small "relevant" general education courses as fillers in a timetable or schedule for the student. This tacking on of technical/vocational with the general/ liberal has characterized the Massachusetts Institute of Technology engineering curriculum, i.e. in each of eight or ten semesters a liberal arts course had to be a part of the engineering student's program. Most recently, however, it has been noted that this curriculum in the most prestigious of engineering schools has not been particularly successful. Indeed, the planning now is to fuse the technical and liberal education in such classes as the culture of technology or language in science and non-science; or the sociology of science; or semiotics with reference to various intellectual discourse, the poetry of physics, the psychology of creativity, etc.

To speak generally, at the school level, the integration of ideas as well as practical cooperation seems necessary. The hope is that this kind of integration and cooperation will develop from multi-disciplinary courses in social and vocational skills, contemporary social studies, health studies and creative and aesthetic studies. If the education of the entire 16–19 population is to have vocational impulse, should a new concept be created, a new unified system within the framework of the secondary school?

The rhetoric of the situation is to assert that while the antithesis between general and vocational education is a bit unreal and many general courses contain pre-vocational elements, it is essential to exploit more fully the motivational effectiveness of courses that are clearly linked to the worlds of work, leisure and living. This requires a wider recognition by the public and professionals alike that a humane and liberal education can be given through courses with a practical, technical or occupational bias as well as through books and more formal academic subjects.

Sweden approached the problem in a more societal context. In terms of vocational competence, labor market demands reduce the differentiation between academic and practical education. Industrialization has reached the point at which it is necessary to establish integrated education for all young persons with both an academic and practical slant. Furthermore, in order to create a new vocational competence, it may also be necessary to increase the transfer of knowledge between the younger generation and skilled workers as well as between educated people in other working positions (both for a new technical development in a new phase of industrialization and as a tool for creating and maintaining full employment).

Economic depression and a high level of unemployment during the early 1920s and first part of 1930s were causative factors in developing integrated vocational education in Sweden, which consisted of vocational techniques (practical skills and vocational theory) and general education.

The chronology of Swedish concern begins in 1918 when vocational education underwent structural reform, which assumed that the practical component of such education should be acquired in the workplace rather than in school. The Parliamentary Vocational Committee in 1952 asserted that the state should be active in establishing a vocational system to enable Sweden to compete effectively with other countries in international trade. The same committee in 1966, 67 declared that all students should have the same educational opportunities whether their courses are primarily academic or predominantly practical.

The consequences of this assertion was to reorganize the external structure of the secondary school with the *gymnasium*, the continuation school and vocational school brought together in a new comprehensive system with 16 different subject areas. Vocational education was to be structured in broad, initial blocks giving pupils all-round instruction in specific groups of subjects during their first year, and thereafter these groups were to be linked to "clusters" of specific vocations, one of which was to be selected as the focus for the second year. During the first year the practical vocational would occupy two-thirds o the total time. It was expected that 35 % of the 16-year-old group would embark on vocationally oriented courses, 30 % in the *gymnasium* and 20 % in the continuation school.

The process of vocational education was first to cover a subject area and the gradually specialize to a more specific occupation.

In the structural reform of 1968 vocational education was viewed as combining adjustment to the second phase of industrialization and response to social demand for greater equality between various kinds of vocational education and between the vocational and academic education systems. The reform also reflected a change from craft-oriented skills and organization to more modern industrial requirements.

To restate, from 1960-1970 Sweden's policy for vocational education emphasized creating a system responsive both to the demands of industrialization and to social demands for equality between practical and theoretical education at the level of 16- to 19-year-olds. This culminated in the structural reforms of 1968 creating essentially a new comprehensive school for this age category (the fackskolan). Vocational education was now to offer a broad initial education with progressive specialization toward specific job preparation.

The new emphasis then of the 1970s had two main features. The strengthening impact of vocational education was seen as an integrated part of a general system for full employment. There were growing pressures to provide such education even to students previously educated in *gymnasia*. The point was to insure that every secondary school student had both an academic and a practical education. The second aspect was the attempt to develop a functionalist view of knowledge and learning.

For the United States, F. Hurn has identified two kinds of vocational education: a movement with traditional focus on high school and on non-degree-granting post-secondary institutions and the more recent trend toward career and professional education in colleges and universities. Two-year and four-year institutions prefer words like pre-professional and career to vocational. These terms are certainly not precise in describing such short-cycle programs as tourism, dental receptionist, and custodian certificate.

The current mood, however, is to stress inadequate instruction in science, mathematics, writing and calls for a renewed emphasis on these subjects.

Some American administrators have concluded that since educational expenditures are justified as preparation for work, the way is open for challenges to traditional educational programs on grounds that the new rival programs can produce equally effective general cognitive skills with the added reward of knowing that they are relevant to the performance of a particular occupation—perhaps an American version of fusing theory and practice in courses in Sweden.

While some may view this process as upgrading vocational education, from secondary to post-secondary institutions, others see the other side of the trend, i.e. the downgrading of the post-secondary or university to secondary job level. For example, a recent study shows that one-fourth of the employed graduates of Bocconi University (Milan) and the University of Paris (Dauphine) perform jobs also occupied by contemporaries with no more than a secondary school diploma (1983).

Reading the proceedings of the 12th Conference of the Comparative Education in Europe Society (Antwerp, 1985) reveals similar aspects in several nations of the new integration sought in technical and general education. Professor M. Illes writes of the impact of modern technology on Hungarian education, citing the need for a new balance between general and vocational education in Hungarian curricula. But, of course, the context of a particular region can bring differentiated roles. Thus Professor F. Lunetta shows the different aims with respect to training and education in Northern and Southern Italy. For Greece, Professor M. Cassofakis believes the new comprehensive school may solve the problem of *Bildung* and *Erziehung* or phrased in a different manner, the relation of education to the labor market. As Professor R. Raivola of Finland states, it is necessary to distinguish meaningfully between education and training. If education is to regain its use value, he argues that it has to give us more life skills instead of job qualifications, which can be expanded into broad qualifications afterwards on a life-long basis. Therefore it is wisest to see general and technical education in terms of social integration, connecting individual aspirations and lives to life opportunities and social institutions. For Finland, solutions to the most effective integration seem to be in modifying structures rather than in curricular approaches.

Yet with respect to India Professor G. Kerawalla speaks of the change in curriculum required to maintain a balance between general education and preparation for a vocation, consequently vocationalizing to a degree secondary and post-secondary education.

The threefold taxonomy of education modes can be considered to be formal (mostly focused upon knowledge), non-formal (upon skill generation) and informal (upon attitude). According to B. Makrakis, the idea developed in Sweden that formal education had failed to give a return for the heavy investment put into it. Thus non-formal education introduced an alternative educational strategy in terms of economic returns, human development and national development plans.

Japan, however, has apparently found it easy to transform general education into effective technical and technological qualification. Professor B. von Kopp declares that while in Western cultures the acceptance of new technologies is so strongly linked with correspondent changes in the ideological sphere that the need for legitimization is predominant, in Japan cultural legitimization and the use of technology belong to more separate systems. Consequently, where the Western impulse is to integrate technical and general, this process does not take place in Japan. For it is in school that Japan provides, above all, general education. Various in-plant training gives actually needed skills and facilitates training on the job. The Japanese mode aims at giving all youth a very high level of general education. But while it stimulates flexibility and the content of professional qualification, it in a way restricts mobility in the labor market.

The respective advantages and disadvantages of the different systems of education and training are embedded in different political, economic, social and cultural contexts.

Thus the German system tends to integrate at lower school level (schooling an apprenticeships), Sweden at post-secondary level (including universities), the United States is moving toward disintegration at the community-college level, and Japan keeps the technical and general separate. Germany tried to move toward integration at a higher level with *Gesamthochschulen* but not within the universities. Sweden, while integrating curricula in the universities, disintegrated research into pure and applied (in the 70s it had given priority to applied). The U.S.A. moves toward disintegration of technical and general education by increasingly vocationalizing two-year colleges and developing four-year technical colleges (awarding B. Tech. Degrees).

In conclusion, Professor B. Holmes's question should be noted, which asks whether the aims of what has been known as general and vocational education should be the same. This might be done by relating them to a system of life-long permanent and recurrent education in which objectives vary with age.

Chapter Three

European and American University Leaders: A Comparative Perspective

Henry Wasser

I INTRODUCTION

On both sides of the Atlantic rapid change characterizes universities, now here more than in the shifting roles of president or rector / vice-chancellor. The evolving influence of government and industry and increasing manage-rialism have brought to debate the nature of qualifications and vision most needed for the university chief executive.[1] In the small body of writing on the subject, essays by Guy Neave and Pieter P.D. Drenth have proved most helpful.[2]

Neave, professor and editor, has surveyed current practice in university systems primarily in Western Europe as to eligibility, constituency, appoint-ment, duration of mandate and official responsibilities wherein one gains clear knowledge of what the position presently requires, with occasional dif-ferences among countries.

Drenth, professor and former rector, sets forth the differing functions of rector by first breaking down the structures of European universities into seven categories, then epitomizing the role of a rector within each category, making clear that he favors the operational role of a rector at the boundaries of constituent jurisdiction in the university structure considered as a profes-sional federation of faculties.

Thus we have Neave's empirical linkage of the conditions for becoming and being Rector and Drenth's causal relationship between university struc-ture and the nature of the rectorate.

Where Neave emphasizes similarities and resemblances, Drenth accentu-ates differences by his structural analysis and selects the structure he consid-ers the most effective in today's society.

Data derived from 150 European rectors' responses to an eighteen-item questionnaire and interviews with at least twenty-five rectors adds to Neave and fleshes out Drenth.

But the need for interpretation remains. Neave has informed and Drenth has chosen, but the crisis of university and the role of its leader require further explanation. Consequently, I have compiled and written this study in an effort to confront that obligation. But mine is just a beginning: it does not have the weight of Clark Kerr's 800 interviews in his study of the American university president, but neither is it teleologically designed to evoke understanding and sympathy for the plight of the president from a national association of university and college trustees.[3]

Typically, according to Neave, those eligible to be rector are full professors, although in Denmark, Greece and France associate professors may be selected. The electorate consists mainly of full professors with the ultimate appointment in the hands of the state except for Great Britain and Ireland. The term of office varies from two to eight years (Germany) to retirement age of sixty-five (Great Britain); limited terms are renewable in most European countries.

In outlining responsibilities, Neave notes public representation of the university, implementing Senate decisions, controlling income and expenditure, allocating duties of administrative personnel and supervising technical and support services. Structurally, there may be one academic and administrative head (as in Great Britain and Ireland) or a head of academic hierarchy and a head of administrative hierarchy (as in Germany and Norway). Netherlands has triple-headed authority in a governing council.

Although Neave finds erosion of Kanzler or Director authority in Germany, Norway and Finland, he forecasts future reform which will necessarily increase professional management systems at the expense of collegiality and academic hierarchy and strengthen administrative hierarchy rather than reinforcing or increasing the powers of the president/rector.

Drenth begins his analysis by asking what the functional and personal requisites for a university rector are. The answer depends on the type of organization, the form of structure and the nature of decision on policy making in a university. Each country, each historical period and each political system has generated and nurtured its own kind of university. And each university system has its own managerial structure, which requires the appropriate rector.

When the university is a simply structured organization, the role of the rector is primarily ceremonial with decision by consensus. The rector stimulates efforts to reach consensus. Therefore trust, seniority, acceptability and respect are requisite rather than managerial qualification and task-oriented leadership.

In the university viewed as political organization, the leadership of the rector involves participation, negotiation and conflict resolution in which strength of personality and initiative are necessary.

If the university is a classical bureaucracy, the rector endeavors to oil the bureaucratic machinery by standardizing processes, output and skills and handling problems by regulations and formal rules.

The rector in a university characterized as organized anarchy is subject to coalitions and is forced to tactical responses in place of developing strategic policies. He is limited to seeking stable coalitions and strengthening them by rewards in resource allocation.

Within a university seen as a network the rector recognizes the relative autonomy of faculties in order to increase their cooperation. While he may anticipate constraints and actions, he has few weapons to cope with lack of coherence or disintegration in this system.

When a university is characterized as a professional federation of faculties, the rector has informal rather than formal power to handle disturbances and must operate at the boundaries of the various constituents within the system. Therefore, great care is exercised with respect to selection, promotion, tenure appointments, training and development.

In this model faculties are relatively autonomous, consultation and even delegation of decisions to experts prevail and the democratic process is dominant in defining common tasks and the mission of the university. Thus the base for organization and control is functional democracy, expert power, rationality and the application of professional standards.

Drenth believes this structure, the professional federation of faculties, to be the superior form of university. One may agree with his definition of professionals as those who share power, are basically expert, need autonomy, have high work motivation and seek opportunities to learn for the purpose of developing knowledge and professional skills. But are academics aptly or conclusively characterized as professional? Does the category at one and the same time fit scholars (textual, humanist, historical), science researchers (experimentalists, inventors of apparatus), technologists (computer, laboratory innovator, laboratory supervisor or manager), politicians (analysts, theorists of political process and practitioners of academic power—intra and inter university)?

Moreover, Drenth's arguments appear suspect when he insists that universities are like industrial organizations varying as they do in size, structure, quality, atmosphere and managerial style, but keeping the "professional" at the center. It then follows that the university must be geared to the needs of professionals as to work motivation, opportunities for learning, instrumentalism, "expertise" and identification with peers rather than with organization or university. The university rector or president in this paradigm is merely first among equals in an organization of professionals.

Alongside Drenth's structure in which a caste of professionals led carefully by a professional working at the margins is a body of analysis that reiterates the role of leadership for a university head. In this approach a university president exercises authority without appearing to do so: he leads while appearing to follow, facilitates, mediates and coordinates in operating at the symbolic, political, managerial and academic levels. As in the case of British Vice-Chancellors the leader may have always had defined power and authority which had been severely circumscribed by custom and tradition, but which in the present have been liberated in the popular demand for a president, rector, vice-chancellor as chief executive.[4]

II

Interviews with university heads conducted in 1989 elaborating these models brought richly diversified opinion on significant issues for the university and society.

An English vice-chancellor stated that the future will bring more requisition knowledge, differing from the narrow, deep knowledge traditionally imparted in universities. Because of great expense and the necessary critical mass of students, science research laboratories will exist in some but not all universities. Consequently, some faculty will teach at one university and do research at another, a pattern that exists and will grow enormously. Wider access to universities offering more professional disciplines will be policy. Heads of universities will be those with experience of spending money, i.e. managerial types. No longer will the distinguished scholar with little experience in managing serve as head because the functions of the position are now so many that they demand budget and corporate qualifications.

A Norwegian rector emphasized the responsibility of the university to influence social change by responding both to the needs of society and those of industry. Academics should have a "say-so" in how society should be. If the university does not respond, other institutions in society will, and consequently they will shape the future. Universities in the nation will come to closer collaboration on the budget. A new University Council of Rectors with a Secretary General will bring about tighter cooperation. Departments will be restructured to attain sufficient size for optimal operation. Traditional barriers between disciplines, often rigid to the point of hindering research operation, will be breached in the restructuring required to get fusion, coordination in research. In small countries like Norway where there are no large companies the university may well be the most complex organization. Universities have broader agendas and products than industry. Where industry has one hierarchical pyramid, the university has several—faculty, councils, institutes, and students—with complex inputs. Thus, it is a mistake to run a university like a private industrial company.

In interviews rectors were cautious in delineating division in power between director of administration (Kanzler) and rector / president of university.

One veteran director, while asserting that both positions were a necessity within a university and that one cannot substitute for the other although requiring excellent collaboration, concluded that there is no good definition for the first-rate functioning of both positions. The qualifications for a director were a knowledge of economics for optimum utilization of resources of government, of budget since large-sized universities can easily waste the sizeable amount of money allocated to them. Moreover, he must be able to read signals—political, social, economic, and international—from inside and outside the university, merging both internal and external signals or priorities as much as possible.

The rector, the highest elected official in the university, must represent the university to the outside world, being the chairman of the decision-making governing board. The interviewee preferred to describe the director as the chief executive officer responsible for the day-by-day operations of the whole university. He thought the position was rather particular for Norwegian universities although granting that the *Kanzler* in German universities had similar authority and duties. Unlike Norway, however, Sweden, he declared, assigned day-by-day activities in the university to the Rectorate i.e. Rector and Director, attaining thereby decisions common to both.

A former Rector conceded that even in his tenure the Director was perceived as having more power than the Rector. He added that one function of the Rector was to oversee the financial behavior of the Director, responsible for the budget. A recent source of increased power for the Director is his ability to shift between *Core* (from government) and *External* Budget (from research contracts with government and industry). Productivity demands by the Ministry tie the hands of the Rector although he like other university leaders believed there were trade-offs for the new regulations of accountability. Indeed, he was most troubled that the 1986 law governing Norwegian universities was initiated by a Ministry official influenced by reforms in Dutch higher education i.e. that the government, not the universities as hitherto, had initiated reform. The universities had had only a minor say in the university structural reforms now in place.

Another former Rector in the same country distinguished between the Director handling administrative and the Rector, political matters. The Director has, he affirmed, final fiscal responsibility. If he thinks national laws are being broken by proposed financial expenditures, he can over-rule the Senate since he is ultimately the fiscally responsible person. If he disagrees, he must bring the matter to the Senate. Still and all, the university must respond to the needs of society, including those of industry, and here the Rector must set the guidelines.

A number of trends converge in universities and certainly they are closer in structure than formerly and the roles of rectors also begin to grow alike. Since the binary divide is presently more easily crossed, the vice-chancellors of universities and of polytechnics more closely resemble each other in qualifications and in tasks faced. The movement from Humanities / Social Science to Natural Science / Technology continues. Even the new president and vice-president of the Conference of European Rectors (CRE) are both from Science / Technology with their universities oriented toward these areas. The admission in 1989 of twenty polytechnics to membership accentuates the trend.

Believing that universities in the entrepreneurial phase can no longer be regarded as producers of new, disinterested knowledge, a Portuguese university Rector calls for revival of the University as Ivory Tower.

A Polish university Rector recognizes that universities are more capital than labor intensive (expensive apparatus etc.) and speaking to the issue of accountability and productivity notes the difficulty of such a requirement where a university professor in his country makes 85 % of the wages of skilled workers or essential laborers (miners etc.) when social logic would indicate he should be making 150 % of their wages.

Since at least one-third of university budget customarily comes from contract research (government) the rector must take the lead in developing a variety of tactics for acquiring funds.[5]

III

This section is derived from responses to question sixteen of the author's eighteen-item questionnaire by European university rectors and presidents, which inquired what the university would look like in the near future.

The rectors predict greater efficiency, a lower dropout rate with studies completed at a faster rate. There will be more economical shifting of resources and a higher retirement rate. One president asserts that inter-disciplinary research will be strengthened. Several look forward to greater cooperation with industry and more reaction to the needs of society. Employing more modern managerial techniques, the heads a decade from now will be cooperating more efficiently with industry and commerce.

An occasional respondent will refuse to predict on the grounds that no one could have forecast what happened to higher education in the 80's. Optimistically, some replies anticipate increase in academic strength and communicational competence. There will be new, economically interesting departments such as automation, data information processing, environmental technology and high technology. This will bring cutbacks in several traditional disciplines, but there will be a balance in the new quadrivium (core curricula) and trivium (instrumental courses). In any event, more diversification, more graduate study and more technology programs will be the order of the day. Structurally, there will be a more substantial concept of graduate school and more utilization of regional colleges.

International exchange will increase with Europeanization of universities. Several problems will not be solved even a decade hence such as the struggle to hold research and education in one institution; the effort to maintain standards, the fight to increase preparation for the professions and the danger of becoming a school rather than remaining a university.

A German university president sees more problems generated for the university by greater intervention by external forces such as government and industry. He prophesies a new importance for academic freedom along with the expectation that universities will be "places for public questions."

One Finnish rector calls for a more executive style management for university administration; another wishes for more research on management. Several university leaders request more evaluation and assessment with respect to the university and more cooperation with political and economic structures. A Spanish rector speaks of the university as a risk capital company. Increased competition among universities will require more aggressive leadership. From Italy comes the notion that degrees will have to be differentiated to balance the needs of mass and elite education. A French university president foresees increasing conflict between Napoleonic tradition and the pressure for greater autonomy. A Russian head writes of a close relation to political and economic life and to the town, region and country.

Several university rectors from different European nations anticipate more vocational and practical emphasis, more privatization, and greater use of technological instruction. A French president foresaw universities as dealing with more social needs on a reduced budget and a reduced number of young and an increased number of mature students. Both a Finnish and a Swiss rector predicted the loss of the best aspects of the traditional university system in the 21st century as universities become an inseparable element of the general school system and market economy. Greater use of technology in instruction with a different teaching of technology was uppermost in the minds of a Spanish and an Italian rector.

Several anticipated that a greater portion of university budget would be coming from external funding, requiring different skills of the rector. A Greek rector looked forward to joint projects with other European Community universities and a more European emphasis brought about by teacher-student exchange and collaborative research. At the same time that the several Nordic leaders saw a falling off in discussion of society and culture, so necessary for research in the social sciences and a waning of mutual interaction, one Spanish rector foresaw the university becoming a social leader again and another believed the university would be the significant research center for social issues.

Another disagreement is detected when a rector from a technical university predicted more general education and a more basic degree and one from a traditional university anticipated increasing vocational and technological curricula while yet another wondered whether cultural development will keep pace with technological advance.

A Turkish rector noted a change to "top to bottom" authority and responsibility while a Dutch rector grimly described a continuing struggle with bureaucracy and a Polish rector pessimistically wrote of a decreasing motivation to study and of a reduction in financial support.

Of course, European university leaders are aware of certain imperatives set down by their governments such as the 1986 renewal of the Act on Development of Higher Education in Finland, which declared that the Council of State requires higher educational institutions to fulfill the responsibility to be managed by their objectives. In 1987 the Ministry of Education proposed to lengthen terms for rectors and deans and to increase their authority. The universities reacted negatively. But the Finnish government, like governments elsewhere, continued to insist that management in universities be made more effective and rational as a consequence of augmentation in their internal power of decision. The Association of Finnish University Rectors may take certain policy decisions directly to the Ministry, but the government additionally appoints a university delegation on budget along with a chairman to act in an advisory capacity to the Minister, a delegation that is different from the Rectors' association. It is, however, a special group in government administration, high-ranking civil servants, who prepare the long-term forecast, the "white" or "vision" paper for Parliament and for public debate. Members interview high Ministry officials and rectors and directors of administrations in the universities in preparing, but the white paper remains their responsibility.

The profile of the European University rector / president so far shaped by specific interviews and questionnaire replies may be seen in fuller context when a comparison is made to American university presidents.[6]

European heads served more years as faculty, with more interaction with other university leaders in the nation and the continent. Moreover, European rectos believe *collegial* (rector first among equals) and *network* (collective decision-making among faculties and administrators) describe the structure of their institutions.

American university presidents, on the other hand, testify to a higher degree of autonomy for the university and believe that faculty governance has more influence on the affairs of the institution that do their European counterparts. As a group they have greater length of service as university president. They spend more time on other than strictly academic concerns. They have more interaction with students than in Europe, and they assert that decision-making bodies within the university have a greater degree of influence on their policy than European heads believe. American university heads, moreover, select the *political* (power-sharing with representative boards) and *network* as structures most accurately describing their institutions.

Another comparative study views the particular discipline of the university leader as suggesting the social value attached by society to that structure, assuming that comparison with another society will highlight various aspects of social esteem and value.[7]

Information from a survey of colleges and universities in the United States was contrasted with statistics from Europe.[8]

The presence of state colleges, formerly teachers colleges, may account in good part for the large number of college and university presidents in the U.S. from the discipline of education.

Further, with the exception of perhaps 10 % of the members of the Standing Conference, mainly from Great Britain, European universities elect their rectors or presidents for terms of two to eight years by a Senate composed mainly of faculty members. In Britain, vice-chancellors are selected by search committees consisting of constituent representative, community, faculty et al. In the United States, presidents are customarily chosen by governing boards of trustees on the basis of recommendations made by search committees made up primarily of trustees with limited faculty and student representation.

For Europe, the response is more directly to a perceived necessary background of a chief executive than is the American case in which selection is made by those more likely to be appointed by state governors or social and economic peers to their positions of decision and power. Consequently the European university head is more likely to come out of an approximation of a democratic process than his American counterpart who will more probably be selected through something like a republican procedure—a somewhat surprising conclusion to those adhering to time-honored assessments of European and American universities and societies.

The term of office of the American university president is indefinite, even if the average tenure of office in a given presidency is less than seven years. This average, it must be emphasized, is for a presidency in any one university, not the length of tenure in that title by the individual. American university and college presidents often hold two or three presidencies in a career.

Even after accounting for a large number of American college presidents whose discipline is education, a result perhaps of the fact that many of their institutions were formerly teachers colleges, the contrast of 42.7 % to 1.7 % for Europe is striking. While the percentages for social sciences are roughly equal, those for the physical and natural sciences in Europe are nearly twice those for the United States. While the numbers are small, those from agriculture in Europe are triple those in U.S.A.

Turning to the biological sciences, we remark a three-and-a-half half multiplying in Europe of the American numbers and for engineering; the figure is more than a seven fold increase. For law, it is a factor of four and for medicine more than five. Surprising is a drop for Europe in Humanities and Fine Arts of one-third where it might have been expected that the ancient European universities would be inclined to elect presidents from these disciplines. Perhaps more predictable is the fifty percent decline for religion or theology as the prime disciplines for a university head in Europe as opposed to his American counterpart. The many break-aways of sects from denominations in the U.S. were often accompanied by the establishment of colleges in accordance with the creed.

Table 3.1. Training in Terms of Specific Disciplines of American and College Presidents and European University Rectors, Vice-Chancellors, Presidents and Principals Expressed as Percentage of Total Numbers of Responses to Two Questionnaires

	Presidents U.S.A. (in percentages)	Presidents, Rectors, Vice-Chancellors, Principals Europe (in percentages)
Agriculture	0.6	1.7
Biology	2.2	7.5
Engineering	1.8	15.0
Education	42.7	1.7
Humanities / Fine Arts	16.2	10.5
Law	2.6	10.0
Medicine	2.4	12.0
Physical or Natural Science	5.1	19.0
Religion or Theology	7.9	3.8
Other	6.2	6.3
	2105 replies	346 replies

It seems clear that in Europe the favored disciplines for university heads are in the sciences—pure and applied—and in the professions—law and medicine. A preliminary conclusion, therefore, is that European universities, at least in so far as their elective choices and disciplines of university rectors are concerned, are more responsive to the changing social, economic and technical needs of post-industrial society than are American universities.

Of course, it is likely that the American president has a much larger managerial and technical staff than his European counterpart and thus may manage the business of his university with greater efficiency, if not vision. What remains is that given the key position of policy determination with respect to the social values of a society and in relation to economic development, the European university leader appears to be more qualified by reason of his discipline of research and education than his American peer. In addition, it may be that being elected by a Senate may bring the European university leader closer to the main trends of society than being selected by an appointed governing board.

A common theme for recent international conferences on university governance has been that the role of university head, formerly *primus inter pares*, has been transformed from primarily ceremonial functions to that of an executive manager with more professionalism and modern managerial techniques in central university administration. Indeed, for example, the President of the Republic of Turkey foresaw the university of the future as an organization continuously interacting with all sections of society and using its accumulated knowledge as well as its physical and manpower resources in an entrepreneurial approach within an atmosphere of academic freedom but administered according to the principles of modern management.

These optimistic phrases are matched by the master of Merton College who notes British universities' significant achievement in creating a genuine profession of academic administrators who see their role not as one of "managing" or "directing" academic staff but as one of promoting conditions in which academic staff can best work. Helsinki University's Chancellor also believes in good intentions, declaring that governments have realized that increased efficiency can only be reached if centralized control of universities is loosened. This functionalism continues with an American university president assigning major responsibility to governing board of trustees composed of citizens representing national and regional interests "accountable to society at large." Buffers against political intervention, the board of trustees is the advocate and conservator of the university, operating only at the policy level, leaving management to the appointed executives.[9]

For the United States, discrimination between the roles of governing boards of trustees and university presidents has become more complex. These boards are no longer coordinators or ratifiers but policy leaders often getting into what has been called the "private life" of universities i.e. questions about the quality of teaching and learning, relevance of science and technology, to economic development, capacity of institutions to educate minorities. They, more than university presidents, may press for new forms of accountability. In short, for some observers present requirements for policy leadership have pushed governing boards of trustees into areas, formerly handled by university presidents, consequently limiting the role of American university presidents.

The new language of university heads reflects changed attitudes toward the university as organization. An English vice-chancellor speaks of his university reorganizing its method of internal financing allocation by treating each department or group of departments as a small company financed by government and its own resources. Entrepreneurship in his words is the order of the day. And, of course, in this context, the position of vice-chancellor will be viewed like that of a corporate executive.

Still, a number of informed critics comparing leadership roles in European and American universities find limited power and authority in Europe. Martin Trow writes:

> The broad reforms of higher education introduced since 1968 in almost all European countries have had the effect less of strengthening the president or rector than of weakening the professoriate, democratizing governance internally by giving more power and influence to the non-professional staff and to students, and externally by increasing the influence of politicians, civil servants and organized economic interest groups on institutional and regional boards.[10]

He goes on to attribute the strength of the university president to American society's exceptionalism characterized in this matter by weakness of the academic profession, non-involvement of the federal government generally in higher education and the forceful presence of governing lay boards.

Since 1985 when these observations were made, several developments have modified this description. The increasing impact of industrial subsidy of universities and the complex interaction of higher education and industry in Europe have necessarily focused decision-making on the chief campus officer.[11]

In passing, we may remark that the rush to the unified European Community of 1992 with growing interaction and exchange among the universities of the twelve countries, as might be expected, has centered decision-making on the leading university academic officer in negotiating with Brussels's bureaucracy.

On the American side of the equation, Trow's attribution of power seems off-center. For example, Trow cites the ability of the university president to appoint senior academic administrators as giving him great leverage. In fact, the president's power to do so is constrained by the functioning of a search committee. Customarily, this committee—whose members may be faculty, student, administrators, even alumni representatives—has considerable influence on the appointment of vice-presidents, provosts and deans first by winnowing applicants and nominees to a small group to be scrutinized and second by customarily recommending only three candidates for final selection by the president. Moreover, most universities have a faculty committee charged with evaluating periodically the performance of academic administrators, indeed in several universities assessing the president himself.

A survey of the discipline background of presidents and rectors finds the sciences and professions of law and medicine represented more usually in Europe, corresponding more closely to society's priorities. A growing managerial staff is still of a size controllable by a rector whereas the American president at times appears overwhelmed by the enormity of his staff. Estimates in Europe are that administrative staff constitutes one-fourth of the total university staff whereas in the U.S.A. fifty to sixty percent is the likely figure.

Closer alignment of the chief European university executive with faculty, both in length of his previous service as faculty and in his curricular interests, allows more creative planning and leadership in research and teaching.

A comparison of forecasts and predictions for the year 2000 finds Europeans more pragmatic in contrast to the more exhortatory prose of the Americans, a circumstance that may suggest a more realistic view of power and authority in the presidency.[12] Yet in both Europe and the U.S.A. there has been growth in managerialism for almost all higher education institutions.

One may conclude that the demand by society for services from the university, for increased quality of graduates required by a competitive job market, sharper rivalry for public and private funds, for more entrepreneurial tasks performed by the university and growing requirements for accountability will determine the functions of the university head in Europe and the U.S.A. But differences in history, style, tradition, and social and political purpose will continue to make comparison of university leaders useful in confronting the dilemmas of higher education.

NOTES

1. Information from relevant literature, interviews, questionnaires and conference reports are utilized in this paper.

2. See Guy Neave, "The Making of the Executive Head. The Process of Defining Institutional Leaders in Certain European Countries," *International Journal of Institutional Management in Higher Education*, Vol. 12 No. 1 (1988), pp. 104–113.

3. See Clark Kerr (with Marian L. Gode), *The Many Lives of Academic Presidents* 1986.

4. The second and third parts of this study are devoted to recording and analyzing opinion and information gathered from interviews with European university presidents, vice-chancellors and rectors, the author's questionnaire sent to European and American university leaders and data taken from an American Council of Education report (1987) and the European Rectors Conference directory (1984).

5. These interviews were conducted personally by the author at the European Rectors' Conference (Durham 1989), University or Reading Fulbright Conference (1989) and at the Universities of Bergen, Helsinki, Oslo, Turku, Abo Academy, Swedish and Finnish Graduate Schools of Economic, University of Oldenburg 1990.

6. This comparison is developed from the results of information gathered from responses to eighteen questions by approximately 300 presidents, vice-chancellors, rectors, principals with roughly half from European as previously cited and half from American universities.

7. See Wasser, *Higher Education in Europe*, Vol. XIV, No. 1 (1989), pp. 86–88.

8. The American project, undertaken by the American Council of Education in 1987, brought 2,105 responses. The data of 346 European institutions were taken from the 1984 directory published by the Standing Conference of Rectors, Presidents, Vice-Chancellors and Principals of the European Universities.

9. See *Proceedings* January 1989 Conference in Ankara, Turkey, held under the patronage of the O.E.C.D.

10. Martin Trow, "Comparative Reflections on Leadership in Higher Education," *European Journal of Education*, Vol. 20, Nos. 2–3, p. 146.

11. See Henry Wasser, "Changes in the European University: From Traditional to Entrepreneurial," *Higher Education Quarterly* Vol. 44, No. 2 (Spring 1990), pp. 110–122.

12. It is instructive that Trow in assigning four dimensions to academic leadership—symbolic, political, managerial and academic, which he later in the essay changes to symbolic, political, intellectual and administrative—does not compare them in value or importance. In this omission he is probably reflecting accurately the views of American university presidents whose published introspections often consist of rhetorically intermixing all four dimensions.

Chapter Four

Economic Impact of Staten Island Community College

By Solidelle Fortier and Henry Wasser

Explanations occur after the fact. A new enterprise more clearly reveals its purpose by subsequent history than by announced intentions at the time of undertaking. Our aim, therefore, is to build our narrative on a statistical overview from which we shall develop some conclusions about the employment implications of a community college based on the experience of one such unit of the City University of New York in Staten Island. The Community College of Staten Island was the first of the community colleges authorized by the state to be established under the Board of Higher Education of the City University of New York.

Any enterprise competes for scarce resources. It would be a mistake, therefore, to ignore the immediate employment effects of higher education expenditure while hastening to justify its long-range functions. The jury is still out on whether investment in training benefits the person being trained, the community at large, or the employer of the trained person. Nevertheless, most considerations of investment in education examine its capital growth features while ignoring the initial choice implied in its selection over some other form of public expenditure or making no choice at all. Nor do we agree with the statement of the economic impact model developed by the Association of Community College Governing Boards, that an impact study is necessary only to justify expenditure to the public authorities by arguing for the primary and multiplier effects of the income paid to college personnel. The revealed preference for establishing a college is made in the political process through which such an institution is eventually commissioned. This preference is the justification for public expenditure. That is not to say that its establishment does not create jobs both at the college and secondarily in industries through the demand created by wages and salaries paid to college personnel. In this sense, it can be approached like any other industry and its economic impact can then be evaluated.

Staten Island is the smallest of the five counties or boroughs, which comprise New York City. In 1970, the year we have selected for our study, the population numbered 295,400 out of a total 7,895,600 City inhabitants. With a payroll budget of about $13,272,000 in 1971, the Community College was a major employer in the county, surpassed only by chemical manufacturing, hospitals, and public utilities in the private sector. Its payroll added some 4.1% to the private payrolls as reported in *County Business Patterns*, a publication of the U.S. Department of Commerce. This sum amounted to about one percent of the county total personal income of $13,500,000,000. The College was the largest single employer in higher education there. A four-year college under Lutheran auspices, a small private Catholic college, and an upper division unit of the City University of New York completed the college and university establishments reported for the Island.

In 1970, the College employed some 240 professional staff, 185 clerical staff, 40 craft and other maintenance or custodial workers, and over 30 in food service. Many of the professional staff were probably recruited from outside the county, although most eventually resided there. The rest were local residents. The census report on the occupations of the experienced workers who were unemployed in 1970 appears in Table 4.1.

Workers were available to increase employment without pushing up wages by bidding them away from other employers. However, the employment problems of Staten Island cannot be measured with reference to the unemployed in 1970. The rate of unemployment was very low. For each of the three decennial census years from 1960 to 1980, the rate was lower than that for the U.S. and the City. In 1970, it stood at 2.8%, which is compatible with frictional unemployment or, in other words, no significant unemployment. It would be tempting to attribute this happy situation to the founding in 1956 of

Table 4.1. Number [un]employed vs. Percent Distribution in Different Industries

	Number [Un??]employed	% Distribution
Professionals	365	12.5
Sales	119	4.1
Clerical	637	21.9
Operatives	649	22.3
Crafts and kind	442	15.2
Laborers	299	10.3
Service	281	9.7
Other	117	4.0

the Community College. We intend to argue the case, although it is difficult
to prove.

The challenge for employment was potential rather than actual, and it was
just this challenge to which the College responded. The loss of manufacturing jobs affecting the City was felt heavily in Staten Island, where jobs in
manufacturing dropped sharply from 9,200 in 1960 to 3,900 in 1980. The following table illustrates the problem by pointing up the shifts in industrial employment that took place between 1960 and 1980. Manufacturing, which employed 16,492 of the Island's residents in 1960, constituted 20.3% of its total
employment. This percentage fell to 14.2% in the next decade, or 15,973 jobs,
and by 1980 to 10.1%, or 14, 727 jobs. The shift that was taking place was
notably into service sector jobs whose share rose from 21.3% to 30.3%
(17,282 to 44,012), 1960–1980, and finance, insurance, and real estate whose
share rose from 11.1% to 17.2% (8,972 to 25,014), 1960–1980. We have produced tables to show the detail of change for industries within the manufacturing and service sectors.

We discover that within the general loss of manufacturing employment
there are some exceptions, notably (1) electrical equipment, (2) machinery
except electrical under which computers are classified, and finally (3) printing and publishing. The latter increase points up the notion that we have ad-
dressed early on in this paper: that is, the potential for employment created by
the provision for education. In this case, the increases in printing and publishing reflect the derived demand for books, particularly textbooks. The detail table for services shows the increased employment within education for
Staten Island residents. Hospitals and business services, which comprise not

Table 4.2.   Employment Profile by Industry of Staten Island Residents from Census Data 1960

	Distribution	%
Employed total	81,173	
Construction	4,636	.057
Manufacturing	16,492	.203	20.3
Transportation / Communications / Electric, Gas, Sanitary Services	10,915	.134
Wholesale, retail trade	11,513	.142
Finance / Insurance / Real Estate	8,972	.111	11.1
Services	17,282	.213	21.3
Public Administration	6,953	.085
Miscellaneous or not reported		.054
Total		1.00

Table 4.3.   1970 Employment Profile

	Distribution	%
Employed total	112,075		
Construction	6.016	.054	
Manufacturing	15,973	.142	14.2
Transportation / Communications /			
Electric, Gas, Sanitary Services	14,889	.132	
Wholesale, retail trade	17,032	.151	
Finance / Insurance / Real Estate	8,972	.153	15.3
Services	17,282	.265	26.5
Public Administration	6,953	.096	

Table 4.4.   1980 Employment Profile

	Distribution	%
Employed total	145,488		
Construction	5,742	.039	
Manufacturing	14,727	.101	10.1
Transportation / Communications /			
Electric, Gas, Sanitary Services	19,555	.134	
Wholesale, retail trade	23,502	.162	
Finance / Insurance / Real Estate	25,014	.172	17.2
Services	44,012	.303	30.3
Public Administration	12,452	.086	

Table 4.5.   Changes in Manufacturing Employment of Staten Island Residents from 1960 to 1980

	1960	1970	% change
Furniture and fixtures	236	204	−13.5
Metals	1,514	1,317	−13.00
Machinery except electrical	703	752	+6.9
Electrical machinery	1,020	1,000	−2.0
Transportation equipment	1,604	960	−4.0
Other durable goods	1,909	1,676	−12.2
Food and kindred products	1,603	1,095	−31.7
Textile mill products	2,728	2,876	+5.4
Printing and publishing	1,666	2,305	+38.7
Chemicals	2,449	1,755	−28.3
Not elsewhere classified	1,060	2,033	+91.8
	16,492	15,973	

Table 4.6.   Percent Change by Industry

	1970	1980	% change
Furniture and fixtures	207	318	+53.6
Metals	1,317	884	−32.9
Machinery except electrical	752	993	+32.0
Electrical machinery	1,000	1,178	+17.8
Transportation equipment	960	929	−3.2
Other durable goods	1,676	1,465	−5.3
Food and kindred products	1,095	1,172	−7.0
Textile mill products	2,876	2,477	−13.9
Printing and publishing	2,305	2,862	+24.2
Chemicals	1,755	1,671	−4.8
Not elsewhere classified	2,033	778	−6.17
	16,492	15,973	

only computer services but also research and development labs, advertising, and temporary help agencies, were increasing substantially.

We have finally arrived at what might normally have been our starting point had we not wanted to begin with the notion that the school itself can be regarded as an enterprise offering employment potential just as does any other capital producing enterprise. To our credit as human beings it is still distasteful to regard schooling in its economic functions alone, but it is necessary to recall that scarce resources are consumed in the process of education and that choices are implicit in the process. Today no one apologizes for regarding education as an investment in human capital. We have finally recognized what Thorstein Veblen long ago pointed out: that technological advance or capital stock is the embodiment of increasing knowledge.

In the operating budget request for 1971–72 the cost to educate a full time equivalent student at Staten Island was calculated at $2,111 a year. It is difficult to imagine who in the fifties would have asked if the cost was worth it.

Table 4.7.   Changes in Services Industry Employment of Staten Island Residents

Business	1,382	3,578	5,084	80	80.2
Repair service	708		1,687		
Private household	709	519	395	−26.8	−23.9
Other personal service	1,725	2,139	2,101	+24.0	−1.7
Entertainment	459	748	1,029	63	37.6
Hospitals	3,550	8,152	15,573	229.6	91.0
Education	3,136	8,045	10,355	256.5	28.7
Welfare	1,586	2,208	3,118	39.2	41.2
Other	4,027	4,190	4,670		

Although the Staten Island community contributed its share in city and state taxes, which fund the College, the cost was probably not perceived as an additional burden. On the contrary, the funding of the College was likely viewed as a political struggle to divert some of these funds back to the local community. Every other borough of the City had at least one publicly supported four year college offering Bachelor's, and, in some disciplines, Master's degrees. Those institutions at the Bachelor's level were free of charge to all City residents, but there were several reasons other than the travel distances, why Staten Islanders may not have availed themselves of these educational opportunities. Access to the colleges was limited by the students' grade point average in secondary or high school. The students were chosen strictly on merit. This meant that places were limited. Secondly, the population of the Island tends to be rooted in the past more than that of the other City boroughs. They regard the rest of New York City as an alien culture, and for those who themselves have not had a university education; they probably fear the marketplace of ideas which the City Colleges represented to them.

Thus, the Community College idea appears in retrospect to have been heaven sent. It provided educational advantages which would lead to far more interesting work opportunities for the people on the Island without meanwhile disturbing local prejudices by exposure to advanced ideas. Professor Arleigh Williamson, who served as Staten Island representative on the Board of Higher Education which oversees the City University, and Borough President Albert Maniscalco fought hard for the right of Staten Islanders to have their own public institution of higher learning.

Walter Willig, the first President of the College, was recruited from the School of Engineering of the City College of New York. His educational experience during a period when the engineering profession was under a lot of pressure undoubtedly alerted him to the emerging potential for employment in the technician / technological fields. Indeed, the following excerpt from the College catalogue is unabashedly pragmatic in its vocational appeal.

> In the last half-century, the growth of the electrical light and power industries, coupled with developments in the fields of radio, television, industrial electronics, and microwaves, have produced an expansion which is unparalleled in our history. The promise for the future indicates limitless growth as new applications such as computing machines, automation, servomechanisms, and atomic power generation are developed.
>
> The rapid growth of these industries has created an unprecedented demand for electrical and electronic technicians to test, overhaul, operate, inspect, and assist in the design of equipment under engineering supervision. Currently, industry is critically short of engineers and is, therefore, placing more and more technicians in jobs that engineers have held in the past in order to make more efficient use

of professional personnel. This trend, added to the rapid expansion of the field of electrical technology, indicates a bright future for the electrical and electronic technician.

Whatever misgivings those of us in the university might have about the advertising nature of that course description, it is difficult not to understand its appeal to the family of a blue-collar worker. In 1960, 27% of the male workers who were unemployed in Staten Island were in the craft occupations and 21% were former factory operatives, in all, almost half the unemployed. They constituted that class of worker, which most Europeans are surprised to learn regard themselves as middle class in the U.S. As well they might. For their wages had in the post-war years entitled them to that hallmark of respectability, that of owning their own home. Most Staten Islanders are homeowners.

That the children of these families could now attain sufficient education to qualify for respectable, well paid jobs just below the engineering level must have indeed been a bright prospect, particularly compared to the types of jobs offered by the service sector to those who had previously worked with their hands.

Note in Table 4.10 the increase in percent of professional and technical workers, which is paralleled by a similar increase in service workers in 1970. The Community College curriculum required competence and diligence, qualities in which the craft worker took pride. It left to the professional engineer the challenge of being graded on intellectual ability.

The philosophy of Community College instruction was not thought of as innovative; probably "sound" would have been the adjective of choice. For Professor Willig, the College did provide a flexibility that was eventually to modify the university structure by its very nature. Open admissions, which

Table 4.8. Weekly Earnings of Wage and Salary Workers Who Usually Work Full Time—1983

Technical Occupations	Earnings
Clinical laboratory technologists and technicians	$326
Radiologic technicians	345
Engineering and related technologists and technicians	399
Electrical and electronic technicians	406
Drafting	369
Science technicians	368
Chemical technicians	403
Computer programmers	472

Table 4.9.   Blue-Collar Occupations

Mechanics and repairers	376
Construction trades	372
Precision production occupations	380
Operators, fabricators, and laborers	276

became university policity in 1970, are reflected in the language changes in the catalogue between 1979 and 1970. The College provided a means of circumventing the high standards for admission to the four-year colleges. Two-year transfer programs in Arts (A.A. degree) and in Science, Engineering, and Laboratory Science (A.S. degree) offered graduates the opportunity to transfer to four year units within the system at the discretion of the accepting colleges. By 1970 this became an implied right, worded as follows:

1. A minimum of 64 credits will be granted when they are admitted to a senior college in the City University.
2. They will not be required to earn more than the 128 credits normally necessary for the baccalaureate degree . . .
3. The City University senior colleges will not require transfer students to make up high school deficiencies.

Yet the school was not alert enough to the social transformations that were changing the labor market and, consequently, the student population, to notice a statement, which would later by affirmative action law become illegal, in its course description for orthopedic assistants The program, run by a woman, was announced in these words: "This two-year degree program

Table 4.10.   Percent of Workforce for 1960 and 1970 by Industry

			%	
	1960	1970	1960	1970
Professionals	9,372	15,956	11.5	14.2
Managers	6,964	9,231	8.5	8.2
Sales	4,342	7,438	5.3	6.6
Clerical	19,056	30,669	23.5	27.4
Crafts	10,948	14,747	13.5	13.2
Operatives	8,529	7,958	3.4	4.2
Transportation operatives	2,800	4,658	3.4	4.2
Laborers	4,340	5,091	5.3	4.5
Service	9,287	15,679	11.4	14.0

is designed to prepare young *men* for a career in orthopedic assisting" (our italics). IT is interesting to note once again, as in the previously cited course description, the division of labor created by technological advances, which separated the theoretician from the more routine aspects of his work and created jobs in the interstices.

It is apparent that the great fear of unemployment from automation, which had characterized the 40's and 50's, had not been realized in the form that was anticipated. There were obviously shortages in the supply of professional labor, which were being handled by preparing subprofessionals. The pioneering work of Jan Tinbergen and Ragner Frisch in input-output analysis had by the 1950's and 60's begun to enable economists to make better-informed industrial activity projections in order to identify demand. The result improved the ability to plan for the job market. Wassily Leontieff had been hired as a consultant with the Bureau of Labor Statistics for its job outlook program. The government had sponsored this program to enable World War II veterans to prepare for civilian employment as the specter of the great Depression continued to haunt the administration in the immediate post-war years. But by the 60's unemployment was less the problem than keeping up with technological advances. The Federal Government had entered the realm of education, a former preserve of the States, when in response to Sputnik; it created the National Defense Act Scholarships. The lessons of technological obsolescence were difficult ones for Americans who had always regarded themselves as in the forefront of applied science.

Engineering schools were rethinking their curriculum to provide for better basic or general education and less specific training so that its graduates would be able to encompass change. Professor Willig as a professor in a leading school of engineering undoubtedly foresaw that technical preparation in

Table 4.11.   Civilian Employment in Occupations with 25,000 Workers or More, Actual 1979, 1982, and Projected 1995. Projections Are Shown for the Moderate Trend of Three Sets of Assumptions Made by the Bureau of Labor Statistics.

	Employment in the 000's			%	%
	1979	*1982*	*1985*	*79–95*	*82–95*
Engineering and science technicians	1,227	1,243	1,661	35	34
Civil engineering technicians	32	35	58	82	34
Electrical and electronic technicians	350	366	589	68	61
Industrial engineering technicians	33	27	35	7	29
Mechanical Engineering technicians	47	48	72	55	5
Medical laboratory technologists	92	103	150	64	46
Nurse (Registered)	1,165	1,312	1,954	68	49

a university setting prepared the student for future adaptability in a manner that could not be encompassed in the traditional technical institute. That he had found a suitable environment is supported by the fact that State Islanders comprised 192 of the 3,387 licensed professional engineers in New York City, a much larger proportion than could have been predicted from the population. The occupations Willig chose for his two year terminal programs are those which even in the March, 1984, Bureau of Labor Statistics projections are continuing to show a better than average outlook.

A.A.S. PROGRAMS IN 1970

Applied Language Studies (Spanish)
Business (Career)
Business (Transfer)
Civil Technology
Electrical Technology
Electro-Mechanical Technology
Medical Lab Technology
Nursing

The outlook as a whole is for an increase of 26% in all occupations between '79 and '95 and 35% from '82 to '95.

Professional and technical workers had been the fastest growing occupations in 1960. By 1975 the projections made in the 1960's were anticipating a growth of 73% from 1960 in their occupations. Surveys made by the Bureau of Labor Statistics in 1954 and again in 1964 had concluded that the major stimulus to the growing employment of scientists and engineers and to their increasing proportion of total employment in many industries had bee the rapid increase in funds spent for research and development, especially by the Federal Government. New stimulus to these Government supported labs is currently expected to result from a proposed change in policy. Until now, the Government had not permitted the patenting of innovations in a laboratory funded by the public but that policy is about to change. The change is expected to spur interest again in applied research.

The population of Staten Island appears to be preparing for increasing professionalism. In the 1980 census 19,918 or almost 20% of the total population of 3 years or older enrolled in school, were enrolled in college. In 1970, 9,883 were enrolled o 12% of the school population. In 1960 the figures were respectively 3,574 and 6.6%. The three census years showed the number of men

Table 4.12.   College Degrees by Decade

1960	1970	1980	
8,747	13,176	30,401	Men and women 25+ who completed 1–3 years of college only
128,119	161,403	209,864	Men and women 25+
6.8	8.2	14.5	Percent

and women over 25 who had completed only between one and three years of college, basic[ally] the Community College population.

Note the increasing population of mature adults in the twenty-year period. Over the same time interval, New York City was registering population losses. The difference in trend attests to the general economic health of the Borough when viewed in the light of a relatively lower unemployment rate.

A study of recent alumni of the College of Staten Island argues for the importance for the job market of the type of education provided by this Community College. During the financial problems of New York City a few years back Staten Island Community College was merged with Richmond College, an upper division unit, to form the College of Staten Island. It has, however, retained its associate degree program. A survey conducted in 1979 asked the question of how long it took to find full-time employment upon completing school.

The results point to the job opportunity effectiveness of the two-year programs of the Staten Island Community College, since 1975, the two-year short-cycle component of the College of Staten Island.

Table 4.13.   Job Effectiveness: Associate Degree vs. Bachelor's Degree

	Associate Degree		Bachelor's Degree	
	Numbers	*Percent*	*Percent*	*Numbers*
Had job before graduation	155	49.3	55.6	115
2 months or less	101	32.1	24.2	50
3 to 6 months	41	13.1	10.7	22
7 months to 1 year	11	3.5	7.2	15
Over 1 year	3	1.0	1.9	4
N.A.	3	1.0	.5	1

Chapter Five

Henry Adams: American Intellectual

By Henry Wasser

This study constitutes a search among definitions of intellectuals, family characteristics, epistolatory citations, comparisons and parallels leading to an interpretation that most closely fits Henry Adams. He is, after all, by almost any definition a quintessential intellectual.

Cognizant of multiple approaches to definition and description, one begins by establishing eight types of intellectuals—creator, systematizer, contributor, polemicist, scholar, disseminator, investigator, and theorizer—which can be subsumed in four units—creator, critic, investigator, and theorizer. Beyond classifications there are simplified cultural definitions—anyone who deals with words, one who is at ease with the crucial ideas of his time (Trilling), one who pursues scruple of mind, one who sees things as they really are and so forth.

Outlining the modes of *action* possible for the intellectual elaborates the portrait.

1. Action of the alienated or uncommitted wherein the intellectual believes that society is not a field for intelligence and is best left to its own motion, which it deems sufficient for its needs. Henry's sense of social duty was too ingrained to subscribe to this behavior
2. The revolutionary who supposes the essential corruption of society and works for its subversion. Henry believed himself so shaped by tradition and education that he was unable to follow Marx or other revolutionary thinkers.
3. Intellectual as cleric—committed to the objectives of society acting within society as a dissident. This does not adequately characterize Henry's social and political stance.

4. The stoic, existential intellectual who works on society from the outside, accepting his final defeat at the beginning and endeavoring to describe and define society rather than attempting to control it. This is a more credible description.

Other definitions lead also to acceptable simplications such as postulating two types of American intellectuals: clerisy—non-alienated intellectuals—and avant-garde—alienated intellectuals. Then there is the view that a complex intellectual tradition as in Europe has not been formed in the USA.

The American intellectual's natural inclination to merge with the popular mind prevents enduring intellectual differentiation (Marcus Cunliffe). Adams's writings cast doubt on this contention.

Of course, Henry's attitude did not escape scathing criticism from contemporaries like John Jay Chapman who wrote, "Henry Adams was a member of the secret society of the only intellectuals in America."

Political intellectual is what his brother Charles Francis wanted Henry to be. He urged him to be a sophist like himself, writing "what this country needs, what it has not and it will willingly pay for is a body of trained thinkers—men capable of directing public sentiment. To be this you must be a philosopher, a lawyer, a writer and a speaker. It is not a thing to be attained at once; it is a profession." Charles Francis calls for a corps of intellectuals who would exert pressure at the level of power as Plato's philosopher on the king or Plato himself on Dion of Syracuse.

Lewis Mumford, however, saw the intellectual as conceptualizer and Henry Adams as the exemplar. He declared that Henry's profound intuition, his total response to the enormously complex world of experiences (note the complex emotional awareness of Lambert Strether in Henry's friend Henry James's *The Ambassadors*), much of it previously unsymbolized and unformulated, on which he had drawn. The very existence of the generalist is justified by his power to see clearly possibilities that specialized competence rejected. And this conceptualizing power, Mumford believed, was peculiar to Henry Adams.

Along these lines, if America, unlike England, did not have a class of intellectual aristocracy, then Henry could assume only its temperament. His thought takes on the clothing and terminology of the dominant discourse of the age and Henry is political in Aristotle's definition of politics as a moral utopia and as a sober and empirical science.

Of course, the family self-reflection contributes heavily to the context of Henry as intellectual. John Quincy had written that his father John inquired into the why and wherefore whereas he saw his talk as the working out of the practical implications of his father's high reasoning. Henry commented on his father Charles Francis that he had "the only perfectly balanced mind that every existed in the Adamses—not bold like John, not restless like John Quincy, not mathematical, not imaginative or rational but "worked with singular perfection, admirable self-restraint and instinctive mastery of form."

The juxtaposition of reason and emotion, mind and art, art and science in Adams, along with such casual notions that for Adams, the historian, the task of the intellectual was to explain what makes events discontinuous and irreversible, often and easily made, did not lead to comprehension of Henry's intellectuality.

That comprehension was the accomplishment of R. P. Blackmur whose analysis of Henry's mind and imagination has not been surpassed for brilliance and depth of perception. First, he compares him to brother Brooks. Henry and Brooks irritated each other into intellectual motion. Brooks had imagination, like Henry, but he used it conceptually before he wrote "while Henry put his imagination in his work so that the work seems to comprehend its own substance.

You use Brooks Adams and you proceed; you use Henry and he participates in your sensibility afterwards." The effects of his intellect were consequently organic, intrusive, pervasive and even dominant.

The fourth generation Adams indirect in his intellectual activity nevertheless attempted to develop the minds of men in power who made values—the governing aristocracy of which he was part had now to exercise intellect outside of power. Henry could have assumed that society was no field for intelligence—could have outwardly conformed to society's rules while inwardly following his own goal as best he could (as his ancestors had mainly done)—could have assumed society's corruption and worked entirely for its subversion, but he chose to work on society from the outside accepting his final defeat at the beginning and to reveal the workings of society rather than futilely attempt to direct it. In the process, Henry's complex awareness is communicated in the multiple responses deliberately made to every level of experience—the scientific, the religious, the political, the social and the trivial—in history, letters, novels, poetry, economic and political treaties, biography and autobiography.

Henry's exertion of intellect from the outside was the culmination of four generations' efforts to force the pressures of intellect on a democratic society. Creators of balance of powers in American society (they claimed significant influence in the formation of the Constitution) Adamses were never completely alienated (avant-garde) nor a part of the existing establishment, neither so close to power that they were corrupted nor so far from it that they were ineffectual. To achieve that balance, each generation placed its weight differently with Henry's most clearly or purely intellectual, conveying a special form of insight.

In the words of a contemporary writer, Henry Adams was born to sum up his ancestors and predict—if not design—the future, did not care what happened but why it happened and was the last embodiment of the American Republic (Gore Vidal).

It is, moreover, highly instructive and often stimulating to the proposition of Henry Adams as intellectual to refer to eminent contemporary sociologists and men of letters. Pierre Bourdieu, for example, wonders like Henry Adams, whether intellectuals, and especially scholars, can intervene in the political world.

Those who do intervene in the political world do not become politicians but *intellectuals* or "public intellectuals." Zola, for illustration, in the Dreyfus affair brought the authority of the intellectual and the values associated with the exercise of his craft such as disinterestedness and truth to the political arena. The intellectual's unwritten moral code of his trade, which is commitment to objectivity, to probity and presumed independence from worldly interests as well as technical competency, is brought to the political social world. But, Bourdieu insists, intellectuals must criticize intellectualism. Critical reflexity is the absolute prerequisite of any political action by intellectuals. The career of Henry Adams is a most telling illustration of these and numerous other remarks by conceptual sociologists.

Thus, Bourdieu continues, the intellectual must commit to a relentless critique of the use of intellectual authority as a political weapon and of the scholastic bias whose most pervasive form is the propensity to a kind of "paper revolutionism" devoid of general target or effect."

Think tanks have played a pivotal role in the contemporary production of the new liberal ideology that has ruled the world. Consequently, Bourdieu concludes, we must bring together specific intellectuals into a veritable collective intellectual capable of defining by itself the topic and ends of its reflection and action—in short an autonomous collective individual—certainly one of Henry's goals in his prolific letter writing to leading persons of his day. While Bourdieu believes scholarship with commitment is desperately needed, with Henry it would seem commitment with scholarship was the necessity for his time.

Yet there are many sides and forms to the concept—the intellectual has become more a concept than a category. Richard Hofstadter, in his landmark book *Anti-Intellectualism in America*, writes, "Intellect is the critical, creative, and contemplative side of mind where as intelligence seeks to grasp, manipulate, re-order, adjust; intellect examines, ponders, wonders, theorizes, criticizes, imagines" (p. 25). The intellectual is defined in several dimensions—a profession that is culturally validated, a role that is socio-political and a consciousness that relates to universals (Rieff, p. 81).

We are reminded of Henry's near obsession with science in Philip Rieff's contention that the social ambition of science was based on scientists as masters, not as the magicians of the new masters. In a scientific age, scientists [as intellectuals] had duties like those of priests in the old society—duties superior to those of warriors.

By the twentieth century it was expected that in the scientist the Greek prophecy of society governed by philosopher-kings would at last be fulfilled, but something went astray even while expectation was still highest in mid nineteenth century (Rieff, p. 340). Ralt Dahrendorf's Shakespearean fool often matches the mask Henry often wears where Dahrendorf writes that the power of the fool lies in his freedom with respect to the hierarchy of the social order, that is, he speaks from outside as well as from inside. The fool belongs to the social order and yet does not commit himself to it; he can without fear even speak uncomfortable truths about it.

To return to R. P. Blackmur, the problem for Adams, Blackmur avers, is how to convert energy and momentum into intellect in dealing with public themes. In Blackmur's language, the disseminative, central force, objectified in his works may be felt and seen (a Jamesian aim) as the core and essence of the open, inquiring, sensitive and skeptical intelligence, restless but attentive, salutary but serial, provisional in every position, yet fixed up in a theme: the theme of thought or imagination conceived by the form of human energy—a definition of intellectual.

Henry was compelled to take the hardest of all intellectuals decisions for a mind much used and disappointed: the decision that the intellect is truly a force which the individual must use though the world fall on his shoulders . . . It is not a fact but a choice: the intellect, like the society of which it gives an account, is an imperative enterprise. Going forward by the incentive of its own horror, which pursues it.

He identified himself with, and assented to, not American society, not Christian society, not *any* society but society itself. And, of course, to the phenomena of the Adams heritage.

Thought in a mind like Adams was never much less anthropomorphic than the Greek language from which thought sprang; he had always the compulsion to put a human shape and a human relation upon the forces which, as he reacted to them, were themselves part of human experience. (compare Lucretius and Gibbon)

Henry's mind ran always to metaphysics. Lacking the theology, the craving of his mind for full theory and for the poetry of reason [he] depended for concrete support neither on reason nor the formula of physics but on the reason and the form of poetry.

Adams accepted the materials and patterns of the twentieth century, though, as the decorum for his poetry, but his story was the old poetic story of how man sets a value upon life and how he struggles to make that value actual (R. P. Blackmur, *Henry Adams*, NY, 1980, p. 263).

Occasionally Henry did play the Shakespearean fool in combining frivolity and seriousness, contrasting intelligence and intuition.

His characterization of himself as a conservative Christian anarchist was both tongue-in-cheek and serious.

Moreover, Henry could always be most illuminatingly compared to the other Henry (James) as two extreme and therefore deeply related types of American imagination. Blackmur believed Henry to have a conceptual imagination whose set of intellectual instruments more or less *predicted* what he would discover; James, on the other hand, resorted to instruments only to ascertain what his sensibility has already discovered.

"If we may quote T. S. Eliot's remark that Henry James had a mind—a sensibility—so fine that no mere idea could ever violate that. To be inviolate in one respect fairly calls for penalties in another. Adams paid in want of freshness, James in want of restraint. Adams might run dry, James frequently ran off the track. The thinness in James comes from excess of feeling; in Adams thinness comes, not from want of feeling, but from excess of consideration. To make a maxim of it, excess of sensibility sterilizes the significance of form; excess of intellect reduces form, and sometimes imagination itself, to formula; the tendency of excess in either direction is toward the disappearance of subject matter. There is a kind of shrinkage of values that occurs under the stress of the general excess we call sophistication which is one trait common to James and Adams (R. P. Blackmur, *Henry Adams*, NY 1980, p. 316).

While Blackmur's brilliant analysis was developed from the stance of a most sophisticated literary critic, interesting attempts can and have been made to compare Henry to such giants in intellectual history as Wilhelm Dilthey and Max Weber, although there is no clear evidence that Henry read them. The comparison is really parallel thinking by contemporaries.

Those influenced by Marx thought of the intellectual as an alienated member of the upper classes who could transcend the limits of his class experience only at the moment of impending revolution. This action enabled the intellectual at once to arrive at the truth about society and to become a leader of the proletariat (revolutionary intellectual).

Karl Mannheim inverted Marx by defining the intellectual as someone who is free from the blindness of class-bound or official ideology and is thereby able to see the truth and to transform society from the perspective of truth. Intellectuals must confront the irrationality of a world that does not allow them to escape from it.

Returning to comparison and parallels, H. Stuart Hughes had found such in Dilthey and Adams. Nearly all students, he notes, of the last years of the nineteenth century have sensed in some form or other a profound psychological change. Yet they have differed markedly in the way in which they have stressed their understanding of it.

In the older, more aesthetically oriented interpretations (he is thinking of Henry Adams), the 1890's figured as the *fin de siècle*: it was a period of over ripeness, of perverse and mannered decadence—the end of an era. Much of this was simply an artistic a literary pose. (H. Stuart Hughes, *Consciousness and Society: The Reorientation of European Social Thought 1890–1930*, NY 1958, p. 34)

Like his contemporary Henry Adams, Wilhelm Dilthey, Hughes observed, was so old-fashioned that by the end of his life he had become a modern. Like Adams, Dilthey lived in the spiritual world of the eighteenth and early nineteenth centuries; the main part of his own century passed him by; as an old man he found himself rather surprisingly cast in the role of a pathfinder to the thought of the next century that was opening (p. 192).

A more illuminating parallel, I believe, is Henry to Marx Weber, also a contemporary. In Hughes's summation Max Weber strove for formulations that would keep together the sphere of logic and the sphere of value. In so doing, he alone never wavered in his insistence that *both* reason and illogic (intuition to Henry Adams) were essential to the comprehension of the human world. While reality, he implied, was dominated by unreason, it was only through rational treatment that it could be made comprehensible. Yet Weber's intellectual coherence had been acquired at the price of a psychic tension that was almost too much for human mind to bear. For a brief decade or two he and his generation had striven to keep reason and emotional value in precarious balance; it was not surprising that the two should so soon have parted company (p. 432).

The skepticism so central to Henry Adams's *persona* as well as to any of the multiple definitions of intellectual is clearly echoed in Weber's historical views. "The skeptical point of view has been common to the intellectual strata of every period. It is evident in the Greek epitaphs and in the highest artistic production of the Renaissance, such as the works of Shakespeare; it has found expression in the philosophers of Europe, China, and India, as well as in modern intellectualism." (Max Weber, *Economy*, p. 568)

A recent critique of Weber, and his sociology of intellectuals, dates the word "intellectual" back to the Dreyfus affair in France, asserting that the word was first used derisively but later embraced by the defenders of Dreyfus, including Zola and Durkheim. The word has retained the connotations of a higher-minded and somewhat oppositional attitude that were implied in its original usage. The word "intelligentsia"—despite its Latin base, is of Russian, possibly Polish coinage, referring to the large number of the educated class that gradually appeared to distance themselves from both the state bureaucracies and the nobility.

This analyst of Weber and intellectuals declares that his usage tried to merge the original nature of opposition and high-mindedness—intellectual— with the emphases on numbers and importance of education—intelligentsia (Ahmid Sadri, *Max Weber's Sociology of Intellectuals*, 1992, pp. 151–152)

Science, however, may be the key. For both Weber and Adams the universality and relation to truth and fact of science superseded any social stratification or dominant party system, thus negating any negotiation between intellectuals and intelligentsia.

But Lionel Trilling reminds us that the ingrained skepticism of the intellectual applies even to the quintessential American intellectual. He writes: "We shall be wrong, we shall do ourselves a great disservice if even we try to read Adams out of our intellectual life. I have called him an issue—he is even more than that, he is an indispensable element of our intelligence. To succeed in getting rid of Adams would be to diminish materially the seriousness of our thought . . . nothing can be more salutary for American intelligence than to remain aware of Adams and to maintain toward him a strict ambivalence, to weigh our admiration and affection for him against our impatience and suspicion." (Lionel Trilling, "Adams at Ease," in *A Gathering of Fugitives*, Boston 56, pp. 118–119)

Still, Sadri's probing interpretation of Max Weber reflects conclusions and descriptions strikingly similar to those of Henry. Analyzing the nature and role of those creators and moderators of meaning, intellectual is a constant in Weber's work. Weber regarded disenchantment and value pluralism as the defining characteristic of the modern world and was extremely skeptical concerning the possibility of the rational resolution of any of the ensuing problems. The world, according to Weber's metaphysic, is devoid of meaning and fundamentally irrational.

Intellectuals are especially interesting because they, more than others, are concerned to find meaning and to counter the unavoidable irrationality of human existence. If intellectuals in their theorizing necessarily draw attention to the meaninglessness of existence, they will defeat their own purpose. At the same time, the irrationality of existence and the fundamental irreconcilability of different forms of life will defeat, in the long run, all attempts to create any kind of universalistic and rational interpretation of the world. Weber in his own work was attempting to think through, as was Henry, the unsettling implications of this position.

For Weber as for Adams, politics and religion/science were the foundation of what we now call "a sociology of intellectuals." Even if intellectuals do constitute a separate stratum (or estate), they do not necessarily pursue their own material, or, even, ideal interests in their intellectual work. The intellectuals rather than the proletariat have more than any other social class or stratum, the capacity to transcend the limitations of their social location.

Tension between the universal tendency towards skepticism that animates intellectuals and the demands of authority often results in the sacrifice of the intellect. Weber's account of intellectuals in the matter of relationship between knowledge and rule, truth and power, emphasizes the paradoxical fact that it is they who are producers of anti-intellectual ideologies. He concluded that ideologies and counter-ideologies of intellectuals are inherently unstable and consequently intellectuals were too frequently naïve dilettantes. Indeed, Henry was at times self-accusatory in this vein.

Along with other scholars, I too have attempted a definition of Henry Adams as intellectual. The key to comprehensive evaluation is that Henry Adams is an intellectual of morality to whom scruple—in the sense of a strict and minute regard for what is right—is central. The whole point of his *Education* is scruple of thinking and thence of action. The test of the democratic process to him was whether or not the seat of power attracts scrupulous intelligence and gives it full freedom. The final goal in society was the responsible control of social energy. Since the ultimate values of society are rarely detected with absolute clarity, every move toward an education ought to be made with maximum intelligence and should be subject to every criticism one's experience provided. Society, however, in Adams's view, saw the goal as immediate power and values as those of personal self-interest of individual or group. Therefore the ultimate objective, control of social energy, was left to irresponsible interests, i.e. interests responsible only to self and not to society. Consequently, Henry's dilemma was the dilemma of the intellectual to which he brought the entire pressure of all the education he could muster upon society from the outside.

As the *Education* relates, his first pressure was practical political journalism (especially essays on finance and politics; his second was also empiric (teaching history at Harvard, editing the *North American Review*, and his third was imaginative expression to recapture the meaning of human energy and thereby, if possible, gain a sense of unity, both for himself and for society (his histories, biographies, fiction and philosophical essays and, of course, his many letters of self-exploration and efforts to influence those with social, if not political, power). He failed to find the meaning of human energy, i.e. to find unity, but recognizing his lack of success he uniquely described his failure and explored the bypaths of his search, scrupulously recording the agonies of his quest in the *Education*.

His search for unity was not in the mainstream, for Adams writes: "The true American had never seen such supreme virtue in any of the innumerable shades between social anarchy and social order as to mark it for exclusively human and his own. He never had known a complete union either in church or state on thought and had never seen any need for it. The freedom gave him courage to meet any contradiction and intelligence enough to ignore it" (*Education*, Boston 1961, p. 408).

Yet Adams, as an American intellectual, had to have unifying conceptions as working principles whereby he could provisionally ascertain every value to be conveyed to his audience. But he also had to concede the limit of his reason, the limit of his sensibility. His scrupulous intellectuality made him dramatically aware of his own failure, and this awareness is the major drive in his work. To R. P. Blackmur, this kind of failure is the expense of greatness. The greatness is in the effort of mind and imagination to solve the problem of self and society and the use and value of energy. The greatness is in the attempt itself, in the multiple responses deliberately made to every level of experience—the scientific, the religious, the political, the social and the trivial.

Henry's kind of failure and greatness had also been the lot of his ancestors. After a lifetime of trying to control power intelligently, marked by occasional and transitory success, every Adams had endured failure as defined by family heritage and temperament—neither John nor John Quincy had succeeded in being re-elected president nor had Charles Francis, succeeded in becoming president. But where his ancestors had found in combination of scruple and temper an effective termination of useful public careers, Henry found his scrupulous intellectuality enough to preclude a public career altogether. The end of life found all of the complexly and ironically aware of the hand American society had dealt them.

But the irony in Henry Adams has to be considered carefully. Lionel Trilling has pointed out that it was in the letters where Henry's mind could work without the excessive elaborations of irony characteristic of his later published writings. In the letters there was no irony beyond what normally and naturally goes with the exercise of a complex intelligence. (p. 129, Lionel Trilling, *A Gathering of Fugitives*, Cambridge 1956).

Newton Arvin has suggested that Henry as the first Adams to be primarily a writer realized himself most completely with the least uncertainty and unnaturalness in his letters with their enormous variety of ideas . . . (Intro. *Selected Letters of Henry Adams*, NY 1951)

"It is from the letters that we get a notion of the development of Adams's mind, which is more accurate than his own more formal account of it in *The Education*" (p. 130).

Henry, in his letters, also illuminated the family heritage as well as informally reinventing his multiple experiences of life of mind as well as a life of social and travel activity and friendship. Indeed, it has been said that Adams's capacity for friendship, so important among late 19th-century "movers and shakers," was one of the most notable things about him as well as being a decisive element in the greatness of his letters.

Trilling's 1950's opinion was that the intellect of a society might be thought of as a function of the money of society—like money, intellect was conceptual, critical and fluent. Henry, like the other Henry, was fully cognizant that wealth was the underpinning for the exercise of art and mind. And Adams was certain that intellect associated itself with power perhaps as never before in history to the point that it is itself considered a kind of power. Thus, where his ancestors exercised power through political office, Henry, denied political office, was able to exercise power through intellect, which had become in his time a kind of power.

Of course, where Trilling fifty years ago was wondering where in American life could intellectuals fine the basis of strength, renewal and recognition since they could no longer depend on Europe as a cultural example, he answered his query by coming to a grudging positive affirmation of the role of intellectual in the American political and social life. But Adams a century ago earlier, comprehensively aware of Europe by residence and reading/education found Europe while accentuating his sense of despair also to be a distance from American democracy. He affirms this in Madeline's ringing declaration in his novel *Democracy*.

Yet Trilling's tribute, like others, has a *caveat*.

". . . he is an indispensable element of our thought, he is an instrument of our intelligence" Trilling, *Gathering of Fugitives*, p. 128.

"It often occurs to us to believe that his is the finest American intelligence we can possibly know, while again it sometimes seems that his mind is so special and so refined in specialness as to be beside any possible point."

It is noteworthy that where Lionel Trilling in the 1950's along with his fellow historical, literary intellectuals insisted that the American intellectual never so fully expressed his provincialism as in the way he submitted to the influence of Europe (p. 78), Henry Adams and his intellectual friends earlier were entirely comfortable and confident in the European milieu. Certainly both Henry's were at ease in Europe. True among James's characters the Europeanized expatriate—Americans loomed large, but they were in contrast to their self-confident circle of friends abroad.

Trilling continues—". . . there was no reason why he should not have directed the impatience, the contempt, the demand, the resistance, which are necessary elements of the life of the critical intellect, upon the immediate, the oral, the concrete phenomena of American life."

I do not say that he did not display impatience, contempt, demand, and resistance, but only that he did not direct them where they should have one, that he was general and abstract where he should have been specific and concrete. His sense of himself as an intellectual, his conception of the function of criticism, led him always away from the variousness and complexity of phenomena to an abstract totality of perception which issued in despair or disgust, to which he attached a very high degree of spiritual prestige" (pp. 78–79).

Here one can suppose Trilling is thinking of Adams in one of his later phases but also note that Trilling presumes this historical—literary best of mind to be superior to the theological, the philosophical, the scientific and the social-scientific.

But surely Adams though at times showing preference for the moral intellectuality of his ancestors is never this narrow. Indeed, his mind may well be in its multiple concerns one of the richest in American history.

The letters, even chosen at random, display this wealth.

When editor of the *North American Review*, Henry writes: "Simon Newcomb should seek the causes of American society's indifference to abstract research and whether the indifference is only a matter of circumstance which will improve with time or whether it proceeds from some fundamental principle of race, political or social system or climate" (to Simon Newcomb, August 22, 1975—Cater, *Letters*)

When professor at Harvard University, Henry proposed establishing a rival course in United States History taught by Lodge, his student and later senator, federalist and conservative while Henry tended to democracy and radicalism. This, according to Henry, would likely stimulate both instructors and students and "counteract within its range, the inert atmosphere which now pervades the college . . ." (to Charles W. Eliot, March 2, 1877, Cater, *Letters*).

In his constant deterministic mood Henry writes, "Democracy is the only subject for history. I am satisfied that the purely mechanical development of the human mind in society must appear in a great democracy so clearly, for want of disturbing elements, that in another generation psychology, physiology, and history will join in proving man to have as fixed a necessary development as that of a tree; and almost as unconscious" (to Francis Parkman, Esq., December 21, 1884, Cater, *Letters*, p. 131).

As scholarly analyst Henry notes:

"But as the study [Bank restriction's essay] has taught me a vast deal that I had never suspected, I have got my reward and care little what is thought of this dry digest of facts and arguments" (to John Gordon Palfrey, London, June 28, 1867).

Or as government reformer, he declares:

"I believe the very existence of our government hangs on the permanence of tenure [Civil Service Reform essay] which is to bar partisan corruption" (to Jacob Dolson Cox, November 8, 1869).

In the role of writer/editor he instructs:

"It [scientific writing] teaches line and follows the laws of architecture and sculpture while narratives teach color, and follow the laws of music and painting—the complexities of art are infinitely greater in color—composition" (to George Cabot Lodge, March 8, 1909, Cater, p. 692).

On higher education:

"My object [in Letters to Teachers of History] was to suggest a reform of the whole university system, grouping all knowledge as a historical stream, to be treated by historical methods and drawing a line between the university and technology. The form of presenting all this from the 12th century till today in the *Chartres*, the *Education* and the supplementary chapter was invented in order to make it literary and not technical" (to John Franklin Jameson, March 20, 1909, Cater 649–650).

"My notion is that all the universities and schools in America have not the energy now to react against any stimulus [sic] or irritant whatever; and they would prove me wrong if they were to show any reaction against me" (to John Franklin Jameson, April 3, 1910).

Henry emphasized in his corpus of work his Rule of Phase Applied to History as shown in the lengthy rationale (in a letter to Professor _ _ _ _ _ January 1, 1909) published in Cater's appendix where his unifying to law and generalizing tendency are in full force.

"The student or professor will ask whether its usefulness may not be wider and, at last, whether it might not score as a universal formula for reconstructing and rearranging the whole scheme of university instruction so that it shall occupy a field of definite limits, distinct from the technical. In that case, he will conceive of the university as a system of education grouped about history, a main current of thought branching out, like a tree, into endless forms of activity, in regular development, according to the laws of physics, and to be studied as a single stream, not as a scientific but as a historical unity; not as a practice of technical handling; but as a process of mental evaluation in history, controlled like the evolution of any series of chemical or electrical equilibrium by one general formula.

University education organized in this scheme would begin by ceasing to compete with technical education and would turn all instruction on historical method.

In this suggestion of a possible means of introducing order and idea into the chaos of university education, I am inclined to think that only the defects of my old university training prevent my success in making my self-intelligible. The same defects are likely to prevent other university men from following me. The human mind perpetuates its multiplicity and perhaps does well. Chaos may suit it best and history tends to show that all its efforts to think in universals or universities have failed.

Even in that case the attempt to reduce university to one general formula of physics is only a natural and appropriate mode of a university education which connects closely with the theory and practice of the middle ages; it is a return to first principles" (to Professor _ _ _ _ January 1, 1909).

Returning to a pessimistic mode, Henry writes, "My views on education are radically revolutionary but no one cares. So I have always found my American audience. No one ever care[s]. Nothing diverts the American mind from its ruts. Harvard College itself is outside its own education. Not only it doesn't fret, but also it really does not care. Even when I belonged in it, I could never make it fight. Theodore Roosevelt himself never could do it, though he does little but try" (to Whitelaw Reid, September 9, 1908. Cater, *Letters*, p. 625)

Henry Adams's role models or culture heroes are few. He does note Comte, but most of all "Marcus Aurelius [Stoic] would have been my type of highest human attainment" (to Henry Osborne Taylor, February 13, 1915, Cater, p. 769).

He also added de Tocqueville to John Stuart Mill as "the two high priests of your faith" [to Brooks] and went on to say, "I have learned to think de Tocqueville my model and I study his life and works as the Gospel of my private religion."

From the profound to the technical, Henry's mind was always alert. His advice to George Cabot Lodge (April 22, 1903, Cater, *Letters*, p. 542) on rewriting: "the defects of technique are the alphabet of art [?] the mind really reflects only itself." "I care very little whether my details are exact, if only my *ensemble* is in scale" (to Henry Osborne Taylor, January 17, 1905, Cater, p. 559).

Often contrasting himself to brother Brooks, Henry says, where Brooks sees money, he sees power. (to Brooks Adams, April 12, 1906, Cater, p. 583)

"I was chiefly interested in the theory, and you in its application" (to Brooks Adams, September 10, 1899 in Cater, p. 499 (reference to Brooks' book *America's Economic Supremacy*)).

Recognizing ancestral traits in himself, Henry did not hesitate to criticize sharply. "If our dear grandpapa had been favored by God with a touch of humor in his long career! If he had indulged in a vice! If he had occasionally stopped preaching (but only when he goes for blood and slays some savage rival) does he provoke my filial regard" (or Brooks Adams, February 17, 1909, Cater, p. 639).

Self-scrutiny and criticism were habitual. "The two volumes [*The Education* and *Chartres*] have not been done in order to teach others but to educate my self in the possibilities of literary form" (to Edith Morton Eustis, February 28, 1908?, Cater, p. 617).

"An experiment, like this volume [*The Education*] is hazardous, not as history, but as art. To write a heavy dissertation on modern education, and fill in the background with moving figures that will carry the load, is a literary *tour de force* that cannot wholly succeed even in the hands of St. Augustine or Rousseau" (to Whitelaw Reid, September 13, 1908, Cater, p. 623).

"After studying the scope of any mind, I want as well to study its limitations. The limitations of Napoleon's or Shakespeare's minds would tell me more than their extensions, so far as relative values are concerned" (to Oliver Wendell Holmes, January 4, 1885).

Letters editor Cater himself ventures to describe Henry's ability to blend together all the diverse forces at work in the world and point out their simple and inevitable aftermath and to seek everywhere synthesis and order. (Introduction, Cater, *Letters*)

"I am daily delighted by the harmonies of fate, and derive endless artistic enjoyment from the lines of human change" (to Brooks Adams, July 23, 1897, Cater, p. 422).

Responsive to various expressions of religion, Henry is sensitive to the different atmosphere of ancient Greece—"almost complete want of religious depths or intensity of Eleusis, Delphi and their symbol the Parthenon . . . is what I felt most strongly in the Acropolis, Aristophanes and Euripides are perfectly intelligible there and alive still" (to Brooks Adams, September 10, 1898, Cater, p. 479).

". . . my having a weakness for science mixed with metaphysics. I am a dilution of a mixture of Lord Kelvin and St. Thomas Aquinas . . ." (to Brooks Adams, August 10, 1902).

It has been said about Henry that he sought the unity of extremes of emotion and intellect of St. Francis and St. Thomas, a kind of unity which he hoped to create for himself and for his own world or perhaps balance rather than unify, which suggests integration. For Henry, in this view, balance is better than control, that responsibility is better than rule, that risk is better than security and that stability is death. The institutions of society must be kept flexible and various enough to receive and react to new impressions. In this interpretation Henry is a formed an provisional intellect which guides and controls his sensibility without excess.

These Benjamin-Franklin-like maxims differ sharply from the mind we detect indirectly from Henry James's missive of March 21, 1918, written in response to a Henry Adams letter now lost (see Ernest Samuels, *Henry Adams*, vol. III), its substance deserves quoting at length.

"I have your melancholy outpouring . . . Of course we are lone survivors, of course, the past that was our lives is at the bottom of an abyss . . ."

Of course, too, there is no use talking unless one particularly wants to. But the purpose of my printed divagations [vol. II Henry James, *Notes of a Son and Brother*] was to show you that one *can*, strange to say, still want—or at least believe as if one did. Behold me therefore so behaving—and apparently capable of continuing to do so. I still find my consciousness interesting—under cultivation of that interest. Cultivate it with my, dear Henry—that's what I hope to make you do—to cultivate yours for all that it has in common with mind,—you see I still in presence of life (or what you deny to be such) have reactions—as many as possible—and the book I sent you is a proof of them. IT is, I suppose, because I am that queer monster—, the artist, or obstinate finality, an inexhaustible sensibility. Hence the reactions—the appearances, memories, and many things go on playing upon it with consequences that I note and "enjoy" (grim word!) Noting. If all takes doing—and I do believe I shall do yet again—it is still an act of life. But you perform them still yourself—and I don't know what keeps me from calling your letter a charming one. There we are and it's a blessing that we understand—I admit indeed alone—yours all—faithful [quotation mark] (*Selected Letters of Henry James*, Leon Edel, ed., pp. 173–179).

While James's optimism supported by a firm belief in the efficacy of artistic sensibility contrasts with Adams's despair of mind, earlier Adamses came to rely on the moral emphasis of intellect.

For several generations they had thought themselves eighteenth-century intellectuals whose obligation (corvée in Henry's word), was to raise the many to the moral elevation they themselves had attained. But they measured the many in terms of their own ideals, their own self-image as intellectuals. Henry could write in the *History of the United States*—the Battle of New Orleans has always held an undue place in popular interest. I regard any concession to popular illusions as a blemish. But just as I abandoned so large a place to Burr a mere Jeremy Diddler—because the public felt an undue interest in him, so I think it best to give the public a full dose of General Jackson."

The context and discourse of intellectualness for the earlier generations were political and moral. John Adams wrote that politics was "the divine science, the grandest, the most useful . . . in the whole circle of science" and he would unite politics with morality. Charles Francis wrote of his father John Quincy that he had mastered "the whole theory of morals which makes the foundation of all human society." He applied moral knowledge to the events of his time in a continuous and systematic way; he knew exactly where to draw the line—and here demonstrates his remarkable superiority over every man of his time."

His father John welcomed the idea of an intellectual aristocracy—". . . real merit should govern the world and men—ought to be respected only in proportion to their talents and services."

In a letter to John Taylor he concludes, "liberty is an intellectual quality. The definition of it is a self-determining power in an intelligent agent. It implies thought and choice and power." Intellectual aristocrats, or is it aristocratic intellectuals, however, who gain power should have a moral sense of conscience which obligates them "to exert all their intellectual liberty to employ all their faculties, talents and power for the public, general, universal good of their nations, not for their own separate good or the interest of any party." This Adams family sense of obligation, or corvée, had moral, political and intellectual ramifications; yet differences existed.

Then there is the brilliant insight of John Quincy (letter from St. Petersburg, December 31, 1812) after witnessing at first hand Napoleon's retreat from Moscow. "The Fabian system [a guerilla harassment of conventionally organized armies] which succeeded in our Revolutionary War, which even in this country [Russia] had triumphed a century before over Charles the Twelfth of Sweden, has again been signally triumphant over the *Hero* of the present age . . ."

It may be said that the ultimate goal for Henry was to create a policy of intellect. In his work he had built an intellectual habitation out of a vast accumulation of knowledge, but his fundamental intention was to define a function for the intellectual in a complex America that had gone beyond the control of eighteenth-century minds.

Henry's complex awareness and exertion of intellect from the outside was the culmination of four generations' effort to exert intellectual pressure on a democratic society. A history of this effort is perhaps the most complete record of intellectual aristocratic or aristocratic intellectual influence in America we have. At the maximum, Adamses kept the concept of balance of power at the center of the American political system and at the minimum they effectively reminded the powers that be of the turbulence they had to control.

They were, given the differing historical contexts of the four generations in the genuine stance of intellectuals—neither so close to power that they were corrupted not so far away from it that they were ineffectual. And in their last significant intellectual representative, Henry, their particular kind of estrangement was not so much a way of renunciation as it was a special form of insight.

Chapter Six

Comments on Method in Comparative Higher Education

Henry Wasser

An institution is, after all, a prevalent habit of thought and as such it is subject to the conditions and limitations that surround any change in the habitual frame of mind prevalent in the community.

. . . higher learning of the modern, the current body of science and scholarship—holds its place on such a tenure of use and wont, that it has grown and shifted in point of content, aims and methods in response to the changes in habits of life that have passed over the Western peoples during the period of its growth and ascendancy—this process of change and supersession in the scope and method of knowledge is still effectively at work, in a like response to institutional changes that still are incontinently going forward.

. . . higher learning takes its character from the manner of life enforced on the group by the circumstances in which it is places.

Thorstein Veblen, *Higher Learning in America*, Introduction

In a brief survey of what may be called a methodology for comparative higher education, I find the following approaches have been taken by scholars / researchers in the field.

1. Locating decision-making structures and relations in broadly differentiated congeries of systems.
2. Case study.
3. Cross-national comparisons: socialization, allocation and legitimation effects.
4. Holistic or single topic.
5. Natural history.
6. Goal-directed political, economic functions of society.

7. Controllable organizations (systems).
8. Cultural institutions with their own lines of development.
9. Bilateral negotiations.

I have difficulties with these various approaches so far as delineating an effective model for comparing issues relevant to integrated or comprehensive higher education in several countries. I note below what appear to me to be a weakness in each.

1. Decision-making structures and relations are sought in broadly differentiated congeries of systems e.g. legalistic and loosely structured; or single or centralized or institutional units.
   Is the broad category (e.g. legalistic) a meaningful, useable distinction? Does it link together what are not really closely related (French and German higher education)? In relating these systems to the immediate question of where the power is located, does it not make for inexactness?
2. Case study (e.g. comparison with respect to three categories—history of reform; difference between goal and outcome; factors accounting for this difference.
   This method does not truly provide for comparison because a system will have different degrees of emphasis on history, different factors accounting for the difference. In some instances an outcome may approximate a goal (Sweden) or be very far from the goal (I.U.T.'s in France). In some cases history may more clearly and substantively reveal factors causing differences (France).
3. Cross-national comparisons with respect to socialization, allocation and legitimation effects.
   How valuable is comparing these effects when the causes are not clearly known or compared?
4. Holistic or single topic (entire system labeled) wherein the simplifying phrase permits more dramatic conceptual or notional comparison.
   The characterizing phrase seems too simple or uncomplex to describe truly or completely a national system e.g. Germany—politicized legalism; Sweden—consensus and state planning; U.S.A.—dispersed control and market system.
5. Natural history—elaboration of each system in its own on-mechanical structure over time and comparison of natural histories.
   This may do for encyclopedic, morphological description of national systems but does little for comparison and insights deriving from comparisons.

6. Goal-directed political economic functions of society—the political economic function of a national society is explained, its goal for higher education described, then compared.
   There is no precise analysis or generally accepted definition of these functions in major industrial countries; thus making a single-country account
   difficult and comparison in terms of one topic problematic.
7. Controllable organizations (system)—delineate a model system of higher
   education, and then compare actual systems to it.
   While increasingly, accounts of systems are precisely delineated, questions arise in establishing a model of systems (ideal—single) against
   which he existing systems of higher education are measured. How meaningful can comparisons be if measured against an ideal model?
8. Cultural institutions, with their individual lines of development, describe
   a higher education system as a cultural institution and compare individual
   lines of development as a cultural institution.
   Narrations of development for each system in terms of cultural organization can be set down side by side with differences and similarities noted,
   but there are the usual failings of comparison by juxtaposition i.e. neither
   a total sense of, nor the configuration for the system emerges. And emphasis on similarities and dissimilarities may distort the uniqueness of individual systems.
9. Bilateral negotiations—use one system to rectify or modify a perceived
   weakness or deficiency in another.
   In this approach, two systems are compared for the purpose of proposing
   a constraining change in one by adapting a feature of the other, e.g. proposing a free access higher-education unit in Great Britain's elite higher-
   education system to restrain slightly elitism, to finesse politically a move
   to massify higher education access, academic freedom, and academic citizenship in order to preserve elite factors in a mass system.
   Fundamentally, this is not comparison but proposals for change motivated
   by political calculation to confront and master anticipated social challenge.

   Similar difficulties have developed with respect to methodology in comparative education. Following the Kelly and Altbach bibliography, we discover:

1. The comparative approach based on forces and factors shaping educational systems, national character and the realities of the school system
   results in analyses which are not concise and in which most space is devoted to description of the harsh realities of the school. The studies have

been weak on one side of the comparison—forces shaping the educational system.

2. Comparison of ways in which education functions to maintain the state and in this manner comparing national school systems has turned out to be a narrowing and imprecise method. The definition of the state remained static.

3. For some researchers, comparison has been really the desire to establish better norms, better categories for data collection analysis. This, to be sure, can serve only as a prolegomenon to comparative analysis.

4. School / society relations are compared as delineated in methodologies derived from the social sciences—economics, political science, sociology, history, anthropology. Here the relation of school to society in the reports has been unusually vague in formulation, not particularly aided by adapting a social science method to it.

5. World systems analysis—effects of international power relations on educational processes and outcomes. This, in effect, precludes comparison by superseding comprehensive national comparisons with a single rigid topic

6. Modernization considered as a paradigm for research and as a point of comparison. This simply substitutes a linear, historical development and compares nations in different sages of that development, giving historical description but not comparative, societal analysis.

A discussion of the state of the art with respect to method in comparative education then seems to reduce concretely to a demand for and development of a formula for more precise data collection, statistics more acceptably gathered and categorized for science. Thus even in the relatively older discipline of comparative education, as well as in comparative higher education, method appears hardly to have gone beyond efficiency even though the opportunity for conceptualizing was present.

Comparisons in higher education must be between evolving institutions and structures. Access, for example, has a different meaning for German post-secondary education than for American post-secondary education because the demography is different and the social context varies. The baby boom (and thus the post-secondary age group) for historical reasons and the differing impacts of war and economy, comes a decade later in Germany than in the U.S.A. and appears also in a different phase of the economic, social cycle of the two countries. Comparison of access policy, consequently, has at least two variables before its facts can be cited.

Another illustration is Sweden where the successful effort to integrate or comprehensivize all of higher education as contrasted to the general or particular failures to so in France or Germany may be attributed to the special consensual politics, consensual evaluation process, and national commission stud procedure. Some would attribute the success to he historical inability of the Swedish universities ever to attain ascendancy over other higher education units (art, drama, and other specialized schools) as obtained in the United Kingdom and France, because of the Grundtvigian power and influence (folk school against the learned "school of death" (the Danish Bishop Grundtvig versus the classics). Contradictorily, others say that the success was the result of the weakness and smallness of the other higher education units as compared to the universities, permitting any university change to prevail. However, the somewhat more equalizing of power and distribution of wealth in Scandinavia than in Western Europe may be related to the successful integration, even radical change, in Swedish higher education.

It is stated that the German higher education system is highly influenced directly by civil servants in the bureaucracy and indirectly since most elected legislators and cabinet officials are of the civil servant caste. Administrative officials within higher education especially in the increasingly powerful position of chancellors are usually from the same social grouping. Most laws and regulations governing the universities are written and implemented by civil servants, an especially important circumstance since laws govern universities in Germany to a greater extent than in other Western industrial nations. To be sure, the traditional universities have successfully resisted actual laws, for example the law describing the function and objectives of *Gesamthochschulen* reads much more decisively than reality has worked out for them.

In further illustrations of national contexts the United Kingdom might be cited where the high civil servant caste introduced the binary system probably to ward off pressures from the 1960s, which would have sharply expanded or massified British universities.

One may assume that the coming to power in France of Mitterand with a large number of newly elected deputies being teachers affected the educational system. Already laws prepared against aid to private education, and devolution or decentralization of the educational system after many unsuccessful attempts since the 1960s were possible.

Evolving contextual analysis then, as Veblen's words suggest, would be a starting point for comparison. The constant differing changes within nations would be encompassed. The second necessity is an exact definition of an educational system.

Does a system simply come to exist, as Margaret Archer says, by cross-cut generalizations which can be made about a combination of groups, material interests and cultural switchmen whose consequence was the emergence of educational systems?

Is an educational system basically a by-product of an evolved national history?

Or is an educational system an elaboration over time of the system's own structure but whose outlines or structures are fundamentally the same for each nation whose foundations, objectives, power distribution and so forth vary according to changing national contexts?

Adhering to the last proposition makes it possible to establish major structural features for an integrated higher education as common for several nations while pursuing the changing functions, objectives, content, methods, power loci as influenced by the differing evolving contexts for each country. And in this fashion perhaps a more effective, "rolling" method of comparison within national higher education systems may be attained.

Chapter Seven

Veblen and Fitzgerald—*Absentee Ownership* and *The Great Gatsby*

By Solidelle Fortier and Henry Wasser

Juxtaposing fellow Minnesotans Thorsten Veblen and F. Scott Fitzgerald offers a unique insight into American culture and society. Veblen is likely the most underestimated theorist in American intellectual history while Fitzgerald is probably the most vulnerable "golden boy" of American literature. The ironic style of Veblen contrasts with the lyrical sense of wonder in Fitzgerald. The Veblenian sounding counterpoints Fitzgerald's elegant prose.

Yet their most perceptive masterworks, *Absentee Ownership* and *The Great Gatsby* are more than comparable; they are alike in their conception of the twenties postwar American society—one in idiomatic socio-economic expression and the other in simple literary metaphor, symbol, and style. Indeed, in these works they are often more illuminating about American culture than in some of their other masterworks, notably Veblen's *Theory of the Leisure Class* or even Fitzgerald's *Tender is the Night*.

Veblen's *Absentee Ownership* was published in 1923. Fitzgerald's *The Great Gatsby*, in 1925. They portray Gertrude Stein's "lost (in her French sense of damned) generation." They convey the notion of a society adrift.

The Gatsby milieu of immigrant Lutheran farmers in Minnesota was, ironically, not unlike that of Veblen. But Veblen had the wit to recognize in American society the rule of an oligarchy of "absentee owners," who would be Gatsby's undoing. These "absentee owners" were the "very rich" whom Fitzgerald characterized as "not like the rest of us." Their class exempted them from the social responsibilities that constrain those whom Veblen labeled "the underlying population." Fitzgerald's novel turns on the very notion that these "rich" make messes that they leave to others to clean up.

In his use of the phrase absentee owners Veblen intended the notion of irresponsibility; owners of American enterprise represented a financial interest in businesses that they themselves did not run. Henry Ford, the innovative entrepreneur, was in Veblen's view the exceptional maverick in this group. Hill, the railroad magnate, Fitzgerald's neighbor in St. Paul and model for Dan Cody, was one of Veblen's absentee prototypes.

Fitzgerald's novel might be called a tragedy of manners. It remained for Veblen to analyze wherein lay the tragedy. The novelist stated the problem in the final soliloquy of Nick: " I see now that this has been a story of the West after all—Tom and Gatsby, Daisy and Jordan and I, were all Westerners, and perhaps we possessed some deficiency in common which made us subtly inadaptable to Eastern life."[1] Veblen might have agreed that the institutional baggage with which they traveled East was too fragile to sustain them, but then he would have asked why.

Fitzgerald suggests the answer in hints through the rest of the soliloquy. Veblen locates the source in their upbringing. The protagonists sprang from different cultures. The tensions, which allowed them to negotiate their differences in a familiar Midwest setting, were ruptured by their move to the East.

Veblen defined cultural mores as institutions. "Institutions are formed because, 'Man is a social animal. Social life is a necessary fact of civilization'." [Institutions] comprise, "something of an immaterial sort, a habitual way of doing things, or habitual manner of relations in society. Not a material growth through not disconnected from the material or outward expression, which it largely modifies. These habits are not inherited but are acquired or learned by the young as they grow up. [They are] the immaterial things of life, habits, customs [which are] after all the most substantial elements of life."[2]

The Buchanan couple was seemingly so rich that they hardly felt it necessary to be concerned about the consequences of their behavior to others not in their set. They manage to rid themselves of burdensome social irritants almost by chance. Nonetheless, the outcome seems to imply purposive action, if not on their own part, at least on the part of some deus ex machina. Interestingly, Daisy's social origins are more implied than defined in this novel that customarily makes a point of identifying social status. It is her voice, not her speech that suggests a background of wealth that is bred in the bone. Nick remarks that she has an indiscreet voice to which Gatsby responds by saying, "Her voice is full of money."[3] Tom hesitates briefly before including her in the company of the Nordic race, the "only race that ever amounted to anything."[4]

Tom's source of wealth is clear. The family owed its fortune to copper, a raw material in the burgeoning electric industry whose importance to the industry of the period was identified in Veblen. The owners, that is the stockholders, of copper mines were no longer the producers of copper. Their connection was a financial one.

Veblen traces several changes that have led to this result. He believes that the growth of technological knowledge, largely in his view a social product, has increased the scale of production to the point that individual entrepreneurs cannot carry on the "key" industries in small establishments. Engineering management is required. The engineering management of industry, however, is not ultimately in control of the output. The social control of production is in the hands of a business community, whose institutions derive from an earlier historic period.

Veblen understood the economic life of a community to be a continual process: one that required an adjustment in the institutional setting that necessarily lagged behind productive activity. The rate of adaptation to the changed circumstances varied among social groups within the community depending on their proximity to the changes. He did not see the evolutionary process as one of amelioration except in so far as there was an accumulation of knowledge of the ways and means of production.

In Fitzgerald, the people are perceived in terms of their social position, both from their own sense of it and that of the other characters. It is a society in process rather than one of a seemingly clearly defined establishment. Nonetheless and although the social setting is not a given but takes shape through the behavior of the characters, its rigidities are no less real. It encapsulates a particular time and place in American history. Veblen sought in economic analysis the mainspring for this emerging society that Fitzgerald was describing literarily.

In the contemporaneous organization of industrial production Veblen understood that the traditions of individualism no longer obtained, though the mythology not only lingered, but was used to justify the hold of the absentee owner oligarchy over the underlying population. Gatsby was permitted to nurture the illusion that he could "make it" when, in truth, the doors to society were closed to him. Veblen argued, ". . . the absentee owners are working together in a joint plan in a joint pursuit of gain. So that in effect such a corporation is a method of collusion and concerted action for the joint conduct of transactions designed to benefit the allied and associated owners at the cost of any whom it may concern. In effect, therefore, the joint stock corporation is a conspiracy of owners; and as such it transgresses that principle of self-help that underlies the system of Natural Rights; in which democratic institutions as well as the powers and immunities of ownership are grounded."[5] In Veblen's analysis, the interpretation of the 14th amendment to the Constitution that created the fiction that a corporation is a person in law enabled the divorce of ownership from "absentee ownership." The limited liability corporation was a person with none of the obligations and responsibilities of a citizen.

There is no hint that Tom has ever been near a mine; unlike Dan Cody, who after amassing a fortune from copper mining, came East as a roughneck miner. He died mysteriously while Gatsby was in his employ. This difference in the generations of copper mine owners constitutes Veblen's thesis.

Gatsby, the son of Minnesota farmers who, unlike the Veblen family, were described as shiftless, rejected the mundane course to a mediocre livelihood that working his way through St. Olaf College might have offered him. The Veblen family had chosen to educate their children in the New England Congregationalist Carleton College in their same town of Northfield, a move toward secularism and a liberal education that represented a break with the Lutheran religious tradition of the Norwegian community. So that, while the real-life Veblens grew up from their roots, Gatsby, of a later generation, had the imagination to aspire to the grander life style of the then "new economy." Unlike Veblen who viewed American society through the prism of his own background, Gatsby believed that he could live the American dream of reinventing himself.

His opportunity came when he became the yacht boy for Dan Cody, a position that introduced him to the way of life of the very wealthy. The dream would be realized and romanticized when he became Daisy's lover. The novel hints at its tragic denouement when Nick hears the gossip that Cody was murdered and that Gatsby was suspected of having been implicated. The true story is not made clear except for the outcome, which was that Gatsby abandoned by the Cody entourage who profited from Cody's death was left penniless to fend for himself.

His subsequent wealth, motivated by his love for Daisy was achieved through the "wheeler dealer New York Jew." This anti-Semitic symbolic phrase is short hand for the fact that the means to Gatsby's wealth were not of respectable origin. In the Veblen analysis, respectability was a matter of degree. Gatsby might have violated the social conventions but not the morality of the "absentee owner" class.

"In point of natural endowment," he wrote, "the pecuniary man [read Tom] compares with the delinquent [read Gatsby]. . . . The ideal pecuniary man is like the ideal delinquent in his unscrupulous conversion of goods and persons to his own ends, and in a callous disregard of the feelings and wishes of others and of the remoter effects of his actions . . ."[6]

The institution of absentee ownership was causing severe hardship to the underlying population by its disruption of production that followed the war. Unable to earn a profit, the owners preferred to curtail production at no matter what cost to the well being of the community. Veblen is accusing the owners of corporate America (the financiers) of vetoing the production that was badly needed to satisfy the wants of the "underlying" population. His friend and student Wesley Clare Mitchell estimated a fall in production of some 60 % in the aftermath of the war. Veblen was keenly aware of the even greater deprivation of people in Europe.

By contrast, the Gatsby enterprise, which appears to have been bootlegging and corrupt lobbying of state officials, was a peccadillo and probably socially harmless, since it catered to the vices of the well-to-do. Gatsby's mansion and lavish entertainments were an exaggerated example of what Veblen had earlier labeled "conspicuous consumption." Despite Veblen's dramatic phrasing, "conspicuous consumption" did not connote ostentation. Its use was Veblen's polemically theoretical analysis of neo-classical theory. In the benign free competitive market concept, which actuality Veblen was disputing, consumption beyond subsistence is a pleasurable activity that satisfies the wants of the consumer. Thus went the argument that it maximizes the greatest happiness of the greatest number. Veblen demonstrated that wants are largely socially determined and the consumer is under some pressure to maintain the standards of his social group in order to maintain his own self-esteem. One's consumption must reflect in the eye of the beholder one's ability to pay under pain of ostracism. The ostentation of Gatsby in his attempt to live up to these social expectations, illustrates that he was not to the manner born.

By the time Veblen wrote Absentee Ownership consumerism had become a major social force. In the Theory of the Leisure Class Veblen had shown that consumption was not motivated by individual satisfaction alone but that the individualism of the economists was in fact a social construct. In *Absentee Ownership*, he examines consumerism from the production side. Business could not handle the increased productivity of industry and maintain the price level needed to cover the costs of the tangible and intangible assets. The emphasis had shifted from competitive selling to competitive producing. Advertising had become a major component of distribution.

Ronald Berman in *The Great Gatsby and Modern Times* is aware of this in his chapter describing events in Myrtle's apartment. Myrtle is the complete creature of modern advertising. She lives in accordance with the magazines from which she derives her notions of behavior and dress. Berman notes the strong French influence in the overly furnished apartment, calling attention to their courtly pastoral motifs in Nick's reference to his vision of a flock of sheep on Broadway and 157th Street. For, although he does not make the point that Fitzgerald hints at, it was the French who were the innovators in retail sales through department stores and, consequently, the mass marketing of household furnishings. The point he does make that relates the scene to another Veblen insight into social group behavior is that Myrtle is not an emancipated woman. She is a kept woman of the lower orders and Tom reminds her of it by hitting her hard enough to break her nose when she dares to men-tion Daisy. Tom comes from a higher order of the "kept classes." His wealth insulates him from being in touch with modern times. His choice of mistress is old-fashioned.

Tom had been a football hero at Yale and he was the owner of a stable of polo ponies. According to Veblen, an interest in sports is a typical rite of passage of an upper class boy. "So long as the individual is but slightly gifted with reflection or with a sense of the ulterior trend of his actions—so long as his life is substantially a life of naïve impulsive action—so long the immediate and unreflected purposefulness of sports, in the way of an expression of dominance, will measurably satisfy the instinct of workmanship. . . . It is by meeting these two requirements of ulterior wastefulness and proximate purposefulness that any given employment holds its place as a traditional and habitual mode of decorous recreation."[7]

It is interesting to note in this connection the gossip that attached to the Buchanan friend Jordan, the golfer and occasional romantic interest of Nick. She was said to have cheated by changing the lie of her ball during a tournament. This gossip indicates that she is déclassé. It signals that Nick would reject her finally. The question arises as to whether she violated a moral code by cheating or an unwritten social convention of "it matters not whether you win or lose but how you play the game." Her purpose was to win and thus golfing was not a game to her but a means to earning a living.

Jordan is perhaps more closely adapted to modern life than the others. One scene depicts her reading to Tom from the *Saturday Evening Post*. She is more articulate than Tom, despite his university education. Nick, too, is of patrician origin but also must earn a living. They are the go-betweens of Gatsby and Daisy.

Daisy and Tom represent the substantial wealth of American society's establishment. Tom had brought railroad carloads of friends to his wedding to Daisy. The social rules of this class are the earlier ones of what Veblen has designated "conspicuous leisure." *The Theory of the Leisure Class* challenged the economic theory that peoples' lives are driven by a rational choice between pleasure and pain, the economist terms for idleness and work. As in his definition of "conspicuous consumption," the use of the word "conspicuous" describes the social context that drives the exercise of leisure. Daisy is in fact too busy to take care of her child. Her strenuous social obligations preclude this chore.

The couple belonged to the wealthy leisure class. In the *Theory of the Leisure Class* Veblen noted, "It is for this class to determine . . . what scheme of life the community shall accept as decent or honorific."[8] The comparison of the Buchanan couple to Gatsby and Myrtle implies that just as the latter aspire to the life of the former, their very aspirations authenticate the social position of the Buchanans. They are the barbarians at the gate without whom life in the City would lose interest. Fitzgerald noted the symbiotic nature of the relationship of the Buchanans to the rest of society at the very beginning of the novel. Daisy in speaking to her distant cousin Nick exclaims, "God, I'm sophisticated! The instant her voice broke off, . . . I felt the insincerity of what she had said. It made me uneasy as though the whole evening had been a trick of some sort to exact a contributory emotion from me. . . . she looked at me with an absolute smirk on her lovely face, as if she had asserted her membership in a rather distinguished secret society to which she and Tom belonged."[9]

Gatsby's display betrays at once both his higher aspirations and his inability to attain them. That his display is symbolic rather than self-indulgent is revealed when Nick notices that his own quarters are simple. When Nick acts as go-between to arrange the coveted meeting of Gatsby with Daisy in order for them to resume in adultery their earlier romantic affair, Gatsby's ostentation offends the refined taste of this former belle of Louisville. Gatsby is disappointed by her reaction but she is not sufficiently put off to end the affair. The hold he has over her is his own response to what she represents to him.

Fitzgerald described Gatsby's mansion as one of the magnificently lavish domiciles owned by the elite "old money" social group on Long Island. Nonetheless, the setting itself argued the inauthenticity of this French chateau. Daisy reacted with typical upper class sentimentality to the fact that it had replaced an "authentic" fishing village. It had been thought that Fitzgerald had modeled Gatsby's home on the famed Swope mansion, so advertised by realtors until someone noticed it had been built three years after publication of the novel. Nevertheless, to Fitzgerald, Gatsby's extraordinary ambition to be realized in his possession of a magnificent Long Island dwelling was at least to own physical evidence of being among the elite despite its being inhabited regularly by the flotsam and jetsam of the theatrical, demimonde, speculator and spectacular crowd populating Gatsby's parties.

The all-seeing, ever-present eye of the abandoned optometrist billboard hangs over every visit of the denizens of the great Long Island estates to the great hub—the heartstring of American society—Manhattan. Alongside it are the ashes, the slagheaps, the waste, a reminder of the uncreative side, and the sterility of its elite. Every journey from Long Island is consequently a reminder of the expense of the social process, of the destruction wrought in the wake of the dominant elite.

Although Fitzgerald is not particularly interested in the history of his characters or the source of contemporary events, i.e. he does not articulate a historically informed vision of their roles, he is aware of their idiosyncratic differences from prototype and their symbolic function. Daisy may possess the underlying cold, ruthless iron of the Southern belle, but not the will to shape and control, for example, life with Gatsby. Tom may have all the characteristics of the irresponsible very rich but not the force nor energy that brought his ancestors to power and great wealth. His football prowess is of the Ivy League amateur, not of the professional athlete. Jordan's goal may be that of the professional golfer but she lacks the force and the will of the professional athlete. Her cheating is on a small scale, not the grand Black Sox scandal obliquely associated with Gatsby and Meyer Wolfsheim. Nick is a trader and bond salesman on Wall Street, not a producer of goods or creator of wealth but only a purveyor of a product created and produced by more aggressive and independent "captains of finance." Yet, although they close ranks and retreat into their own world when things get rough, the novel describes significant interaction between the Buchanan couple and the outer world. That Daisy is attracted to Gatsby is obvious. This romance is paralleled by a more conventional liaison between Tom and Myrtle. Gatsby and Myrtle have the vigor and charm to tempt the Olympian gods, but they are cursed by Hera/Daisy who, while being responsible for their deaths, will emerge unscathed.

Only Nick and the unassimilated Greek merchant who sits the mourning vigil with Myrtle's husband seem capable of human empathy. The latter's authenticity is a poignant reminder of the profundity of mourning in ancient Greek tragedy. Indeed, the genuineness of this minor character and objective human response contrasts sharply with the inability of the major characters to experience full-throated emotion.

Nick, on his return to St. Paul at the end of the novel, comments on the fact that the Buchanan couple, Gatsby, Jordan and he were all Midwesterners. However, where Fitzgerald saw a dichotomy, Veblen would see a continuum. The flaws of the protagonists were present before they moved East, so that it is difficult to comprehend the important role of the East in the tragedy. Yet both Veblen and Fitzgerald seem to be conscious of the ability of the East to manipulate the lives of Midwesterners. Few people from the East appear in the novel. The crowds that frequented the soirées of Gatsby never emerge as individuals except in their monstrously inhuman reaction to his death. The roles of Myrtle and her husband are passive, despite her death and his murder of Gatsby. Thus the contrast between East and Midwest must exist in the perceptions of the Midwesterners. And so they probably did in the consciousness of Fitzgerald and Veblen.

Veblen interpreted the Midwest through his ethnicity. To him the towns of the great farming districts are the very flower "of self-help and cupidity standardized on the American plan." Veblen thought the analysis of these towns had been omitted from economics, at the same time that they explained much about the economic life in the American that preceded the era of Big Business.[10] Nick reminisces about nostalgic Christmas homecomings from prep schools of the children of the wealthier merchants like his father whose family was in the hardware business. What Nick remembered as comforting, Veblen would characterize more sharply as a "system of intellectual, institutional and religious holdovers." The business of retail sales in which they were engaged discouraged opinions that ran contrary to the "commonplaces of the day before yesterday." The reasons for Veblen's attack on the complacency of Midwestern townspeople are not far to seek. Their merchants enjoyed a monopolistic position to the nearby farmer so "that as it runs today it imposes on the country's farm industry an annual overhead charge which runs into ten or twelve figures." Nick confirms Veblen's observations of conflicts of interest by the snobbish callousness with which he dismisses the farmer. With Babbitt's complacency, he fails to make the connection between the wealth of the St. Paul merchants and wheat production. "That's my Middle West—not the wheat or the prairies or the lost Swede towns, but the thrilling returning trains of my youth."[11]

Though Veblen would not be moved by it, he could account for the nostalgia experienced by Nick. "The road to success has run into and through the country town, or its retail trade equivalent in the cities, and the habits of thought engendered by the preoccupations of the retail trade have shaped popular sentiment and popular morals and have dominated public morals. . . . That is what is meant by democracy in American parlance . . . and it is for this . . . that the Defenders of the American Faith once aspired to make the world safe."[12]

Nick does not recognize that the life he had known is over as he continues to muse on his return, "I am part of that, a little solemn with the feel of those long winters, a little complacent from growing up in the Carraway house, in a city where dwellings are still called through decades by a family's name."[13] Veblen states that the best days of the retail trade are past in the sense that the "once masterless retailer is coming in for a master, that the massive vested interests that move obscurely in the background [read the East] now have first call on the 'income stream.' Technological changes in the means of transport and communication have led to increased use of advertisement, increased size of business concerns, increased resort to packaged goods, brands and trade marks, increased resort to chain-store methods, etc. The market has become national and the monopolistic situation of urban areas has deteriorated."[14]

Finally, it might be said that the East operates to the West as a kind of absentee owner in the Veblenian sense. The main characters are associated with the Midwest—Tom, Chicago—Nick, St. Paul—Daisy, Louisville—Gatsby,

Minnesota—yet for each the East is a control, a contrapuntal force. For Tom great wealth operates irresponsibly and exploits leisure underneath Eastern gentility. Daisy, with her overlay of Southern tradition, acts irresponsibly under the stimulation of Eastern manners. Nick, with an Ivy League education, tries to function professionally under Eastern dominion. Gatsby is freewheeling out of Minnesota but he is influenced to illegal and non-traditional modes of acquiring wealth by Eastern ways and sinister cosmopolitan figures. The East not only influences the central life patterns of Midwesterners; it offers a cultural challenge, which their own values cannot withstand.

NOTES

1. F. Scott Fitzgerald, *The Great Gatsby*, New York: Scribner's, 1025 (renewed copyright 1953), p. 155.

2. Thorsten Veblen, *Absentee Ownership and Business Enterprise in Recent Times: The Case of America*, New York: August M. Kelley Reprints, 1964, copyright 1924, p. 257 footnote.

3. *Ibid*. p. 107.

4. *Ibid*. p. 17.

5. *Ibid*. p. 207.

6. *Ibid*. pp. 82–83.

7. *Ibid*. p. 260.

8. Thorsten Veblen, *The Theory of the Leisure Class, an Economic Study of Institutions*, New York: The Modern Library, 1934, p. 104.

9. *Great Gatsby*, p. 21.

10. *Absentee Ownership*, p. 142 and chapter on "The Country Town."

11. *Gatsby*, p. 155.

12. *Absentee Ownership*, p. 151.

13. *Gatsby*, p. 155.

14. *Op. cit*. p. 151.

Chapter Eight

Universities in the Age of Privatization

Henry Wasser

A major concern in higher education policy is privatization. The details are extensively described in current discussion. Noteworthy is the changing mix in public versus private financial support toward the private. Another issue is that the drift involves transformation of assumptions, perceptions and values. A third is that new, more vigorous competition accompanies privatization. And, finally, important private benefits are realized when privatization occurs. (See Roger Geiger's lengthy account "The American University at the Beginning of the Twenty-First Century: Signposts on the Path to Privatization," in *Trends in American and German Higher Education*, ed. Robert McAdams, American Academy of Art and Science, 2002, pp. 33–84).

The increased necessity for private funding has shifted the cost of higher education to students and parents, to the privatization of academic research both in its funding and its utilization, to growing entrepreneurialism in universities, both in external activity and internal management.

Privatization of academic research in particular has produced, additionally, changes in the assumptions about the nature and uses of academic knowledge. Federal funds have encouraged an ivory-tower mentality about the purity of inquiry and critical positions the university should assume towards society. Geiger has asserted that after 1980 there were demands that academic research contribute toward the national economic competition, particularly where molecular biology and commercial pharmaceutical products joined in a union that contributed heavily to the new university spirit of entrepreneurialism.

Moreover, possessing large endowments universities became sophisticated investors with asset-allocation models, professional money mangers, program trading and other Wall Street strategies.

Geiger confronts the accusation that universities have been shielded from market forces and have failed to undergo the downsizing and economic rationalizing that American industry took, but he neglects to deal substantively with the consequences of the managerial, enterprising revolution in the universities on such matters as weakening traditional collegial decision-making and faculty governance.

Several observers have noted that colleges and universities have found market areas that are protected from public competition. Urban private universities, for example, have more consistently met the demand for professional programs by supplementing public provision with more higher education alternatives.

In this atmosphere of privatization, examples are multiplying, such as that of the University of Virginia, which has phased out all state support for its schools of law and business, making them completely self-supporting, largely through tuition.

Paradoxically, while large public universities are losing state support, their very size permits them to acquire more private research grant support because of the utility of large-scale inter-disciplinary research activity, whether basic or instrumental. At the same time, economic competitiveness demands closer linkage between university research and the development of products and services for industry. As has often been remarked, a key stimulus was the Bayh-Dole Act of 1980, which allowed non-profit organizations (e.g. universities) to own patents in inventions derived from federally supported research, with patent income divided among inventor, department and university.

Since universities encompass such wide-ranging activities as distance, continuing education, technological services to industry, outreach education, that require managerial as well as scientific expertise, they employ professional managers, conditioned in an administrative apparatus derived from a market-oriented managerial culture—so much so that some question whether a point will shortly be reached when this conglomerate cannot be called a university in its historic definition.

Decline in public investment and increase in private funding have brought greater hierarchy but not wider distribution of opportunity to American society. While the number of faculty has not grown, the expansion of academic research more and more financed privately has taken place on the edges of university life in special, non-academic units staffed by non-faculty researchers. This swing of the pendulum has been described in considerable detail, but the complex role of politics at state and national level on the growth of privatization has not been fully explored. As an illustration, there are the political developments in the state of New York wherein taxpayer money is given to private colleges and universities for each bachelor's, masters and doctor's degree they bestow. In addition, the state supports indirectly construction of facilities for private higher education institutions—a glaring example is state financing for library construction at private Marist College accompanied by denial of funds for a library construction at the State University of New York at New Paltz.

Furthermore, the fact that the majority of state legislators in California are graduates of public institutions, in contrast to those in New York who are mostly graduates of private colleges, religious and secular, has influenced the extent of funding for state-supported public institutions.

Governing boards of trustees at public universities consist of appointees who are customarily from the world of industry and business, familiar with corporate priorities that they bring to, and encourage as, decision-making public university trustees.

And, of course, the primary current obligation of university presidents is to raise funds, an activity which along with the pervasive context of enterprise universities, entrepreneurial administrators and managers, economic rationalization within universities derived from corporate / business organization predisposes toward privatization.

Aware of these responsibilities, Clark Kerr as early as 1993 had noted the importance of the privatizing trend in higher education and its consequences epitomized in his conclusion that the major movement had been from "land grant" to "federal research" and finally to "enterprise" university. Heavy emphasis in the "entrepreneurial" and "enterprise" was to come in the next decade. Kerr saw that such change meant greater reliance on increased tuition, differentiated tuition in areas that led to high-income professions, more solicitations of alumni and increased pure and instrumental grants from industry. Prescient as Kerr was, he could not anticipate the range and power of the contemporary corporate / market university.

While higher education policy analysts have been cognizant of the move toward centrality of privatization, a full-length, comprehensive study has not yet been published. Burton Clark writes of the typical ways of coordination within higher education in "state authority, academic oligarchy and market." Martin Trow remarks that the market-regulated system leads to diversified pattern whereas a government-steered system emphasizes distinct types of egalitarian patterns. Knowing that government and market favor a variety of goals and programs, Gary Rhoades believes that academics emphasize homogeneous goals and consequently support hierarchical rather than genuine diversified patterns of higher education.

The American Way, according to Keith Tribe, has always been to mobilize vast research to achieve social and economic objectives, in the process creating a lot of waste and disorder. That is the way, he continues, of the market mechanism and accounts for both the strengths and weaknesses of higher education in the United States. Being highly bureaucratized, the U.S. has comprehensive education statistics available. Achievements of American higher education are then the outcome of complex interaction of market and bureaucracy over a period of decades.

In contrast, the situation in the former Communist countries of Eastern Europe permits the continuing protection afforded to higher education by state funding to lessen the potential effect of market competition and the "global" aspects of transformation. In some of these countries, private universities have been created which attempt to meet the new needs of new times or at least a limited subset of them. In other countries, establishing private institutions has been severely limited by national legislation. Lynn Meek observes that after the collapse of the iron curtain of the former Soviet Union, the victory of the free market continues to be widely celebrated. Similarly, Bruce Johnstone has affirmed that underlying the market orientation of tertiary education is the ascendancy, almost worldwide, of market capitalism and the principles of neo-liberal economics. But he does foresee a growing protest against further ascendancy and globalization of the market.

Lynn Meek has also described the notion in which it is assumed that higher education is made more effective and cost-efficient in an environment of deregulated state control and enhanced institutional entrepreneurship where market relations, consumer control, user-pays and institutional entrepreneurship help to further the universal trend toward privatization / marketization in higher education. Indeed, the growth of privateness within higher education and market-like relations occurs in many countries regardless of whether their systems are primarily public or have dual public and private sections.

Privatization in this view is being embraced both as an ideology in its own right and as a reaction to what is perceived as "public failure." Economic rationalism in this case reflects the belief that market forces rather than state intervention will make institutions more cost-effective and better managed as well as making higher education systems more fluid and responsive to client needs and demands. Moreover, the growth of international higher-education consortia, which, unlike previous networks of universities and colleges possessing a predominantly academic focus, are now under the control of administrators / managers (university executives) who cater to the future advantage of global market opportunities in selling higher-education products. Consequently, the mechanisms of control travel from public to private sectors and from nation states to a much more nebulous international arena (globalization).

The growth of privatization has naturally influenced the immediate world of higher education policy analysts. The 2006 conference of the European

Association of Institutional Researchers, entitled "Who Runs Higher Education in a Competitive World?" is sponsored by University Guido Carlo whose main shareholder is the Association of Italian Industries.

Even more problematic countries respond to the trend. In Iraq, private higher education started in 1988 to create study opportunities to those unable to obtain acceptable average degrees from public universities. In the midst of the chaos of present-day Iraq, there are concerted efforts to establish a private International University of Iraq—non-profit—of which the main campus would be in Baghdad and regional campuses in Erbil, Iraqi Kurdistan and Basra under a global partnership headquartered in Canada. Brazil has effectively formed a relation between universities and private companies that diminishes the public higher education and expands the private sector. Azerbeijan has created private universities, which offer programs new in substance and form. Western European nations are gingerly testing the waters—in England Buckingham, in Germany Bremen.

The dominance of the privatization mode in contemporary higher education institutions can no longer be doubted. Time-tested values associated with state universities seem relegated to the sidelines. While universities have always been important and responsive to social needs, their greatest contribution, in Gordon Graham's description, has always been the education of the mind—the cultivation of comprehension, not simply furnishing technical skills to the work force or accumulating, conserving and disseminating knowledge for its own sake, though these are indeed valuable contributions. Consequently, it must be concluded that it is not what is available to be known that matters, but the ability to determine whether or not it is important to know it; whether knowing something results in greater comprehension or not; whether the world is enriched as a consequence or not.

But these sentiments are increasingly viewed as archaic and irrelevant. A significant statistic is that in 2003–4 the U.S. Department of Education's National Center for Education Statistics noted that teaching staff accounted for just 37 % of staff on U.S. campuses. They were outnumbered by the combined ranks of professional administrators (34.2 %) and auxiliaries such as clerks, maintenance workers and academic support staff (28.8 %). Post-graduate programs offering masters and doctorates in higher education administration have proliferated, professionalizing administrative ranks (there are 127 such programs in the U.S. Two rapidly growing administrative areas are support staff, who are often hired in casual contracts for specific research projects, and the cohort staff, recruited to manage the burden of research and financial regulations requirements.

Some analysts like Roger Geiger conclude that this kind of assistance enables faculty to concentrate on their job. However, this assertion seems problematic in the light of the increased decision-making power supported by the growing salary gap between administrator-managers and faculty. And indeed it is often the case that increased demand by administrators for paper work has severely interrupted the faculty's teaching and research responsibilities. Presidential salaries range from two to five times that of senior professors. Demonstrating how high-powered senior administrative positions have become, more than half of recently appointed university presidents in 2001 were recruited by executive head-hunters compared with just 16 % before 1995.

Outside interest groups, such as state legislators, want to know to what extent universities are transferring intellectual property into the market. They want to know how many patents and how many start-up companies are being generated. This pressure has again resulted in boosting the number of administrative staff. Such emphasis on exploiting intellectual property for income may well lead to the neglect of more speculative research without immediate commercial application and adversely impact disciplines with few entrepreneurial outlets.

This brief account concludes that the dominant structure of the contemporary university may well be "privatized," stage four to be added to Clark Kerr's three-stages phrased as "land-grant" to "federal research" to "enterprise / entrepreneurial."

Chapter Nine

The Costs of the Benefits of Recent Higher Education Reforms

Henry Wasser

Recent analyses point aptly and concisely to six major ongoing reforms in higher education likely resulting from social need. They are, first in brief formulation, diversification of institutional programs and modes of delivery to accommodate the demand from an increasingly diverse population. Second is the necessity to find new resources and ways to finance the growing system of higher education. Next is the movement to redefine the relationship between government and university. Then the requirement is noted to coordinate the various parts of higher or the entire post-secondary education system including private sector by re-analyzing their roles and relationship comprehensively. A fifth category is to facilitate the collaboration of higher education with its different environment, especially that of industry. And, finally, conceptualizing the mission of higher education within a global economy and as a new technological climate looms.

Many defenders of the traditional university in the face of these reforms would probably concur with Anthony Smith's formulation which proclaimed the 19th-century university to be the designated defender of a set of civilizational values as an autonomous institution collegial in style, living by the ethics of academic responsibility and the university to be a place for teaching universal knowledge. If that university was the starting point, then the narrative since then is of decline and crisis. And the 21st century shows a loss of expectations and an inward looking at the past.

But Smith maintains that the past institution was never as coherent as supposed nor does the present one provide what it promises. He holds that the apposite metaphor is geological in which the history of the academy is a accumulating, layering of practice, conceptions and initiatives—layerings rather than displacements.

There is, however, a cost to the traditional academic values, functions and visions in meeting those challenges requiring far-reaching changes in the way higher education is organized, financed and governed—the aforementioned six major movements of reform.

The campaigns for equality in education have resulted in heightened pressure for democratization. The growing scale of higher institutions has brought its own new wave of managerialism and has jeopardized collegiality. The increased momentum of globalization has carried a powerful wave of cosmopolitanism into the academy, ridding it of the more intentionally national project and of the mental framework that once shaped research and teaching.

While instrumental knowledge has always been part of universal learning, it has come to dominate, and the humanities have to make a self-apology and struggle to find their place in institutions in which the managers, borrowing the language of current politics constantly question every course for its utility, for its contribution to the economy and "creation of jobs." In 1980 Lord Robbins could write that the universities are "where cultivation of scholarship and of scientific speculation [should be] carried on side by side." Now the university has adopted the causes of individual capitalism and economic growth as its own. Lord Robbins' compromise has given way to a dominant instrumentality.

One consequence has been the university's loss of its position at the center of authoritative knowledge, displaced by think tanks, private corporations and media companies; the dominant phrases are pursuit of "transferable" skills, "competencies" without content, "marketable" analytical abilities, "problem-solving" and communication skills. Universities have become a brand, students have become consumers, teachers work on, contract, and talk of products, the corporate presence is everywhere together with the corporate mindset. Performativity, entrepreneurship, managerial and "audit" cultures are the words of choice. Universities have responded with mission statements and "business plans."

These indeed are contrasting interpretations of the higher education scene—the identified movements for reform apparently stemming from social necessity and the centuries-old sense of university intent and values. Recognizing the necessity of higher education change, I look for verification of observations by several university scholars and administrators and suggest along with them possible consequent damage to long-established academic principles.

My presupposition is that current higher education reforms have been responsive to social needs and educational progress but that there are significant warnings or cautionary signs to note—costs to traditional university values that such reforms produce.

In the category of finance, Derek Bok has written that in pursuing money-making ventures, universities may compromise their essential academic values. His examples are pertinent.

Assistant professors are diverted from on-campus duties to teach elementary material to entry-level executives. To profit from Internet ventures, universities offer users a chance to take inferior courses to earn a problematic certificate in business studies. Professors may be tenured for bringing in large patent royalties. Space in university buildings may be allotted not in accordance with academic values and needs but in with he size of grant obtained. Universities seek commercial advertisers to sponsor courses on the Internet. Undistinguished students may be accepted on the implicit understanding that their parents will make substantial gifts

Moreover, rewards from profit-seeking ventures are often disappointing. High-profile athletics may produce revenue—but not consistently. Patent licensing for most institutions may not earn more than the cost of operating a technology transfer office. New York, Temple and Columbia universities have recently shut down for-profit Internet offices after losing millions of dollars.

Other vulnerabilities include failure to impose strict conflict-of-interest rules. Universities have at times failed to protect their scientists from corporate pressure to suppress unfavorable research findings. Some published reports from university researchers on efficiency of products of commercial sponsors of research have actually been ghostwritten by company personnel. Seeking profits from continuing education programs, universities offer no financial aid, low adjunct salaries, thus affecting quality of teaching. Celebrity professors are used on Internet rather than the more expensive new technology that improves the effectiveness of teaching and learning.

Some of these vulnerabilities may have resulted from over-reliance on centralized governance structure. Indeed, several models have been created as efforts have increased to find the proper balance between centralization and decentralization, between internal (academic) values and external (corporate) and or market-dominated) influence in the allocation of authority within the institutions and between stability and flexibility when it comes to the organized structure of the institutions.

Ideas of the university as a corporate enterprise or adaptive as entrepreneurial or as a learning organization have been launched. Also projected is the underlying assumption that procedural academic leadership—(the *primus inter pares* model). This approach leads to assessment of the professional life as merely making a living rather than as viewed traditionally as a calling.

For Bok, these aforesaid vulnerabilities may be strengthened by boards of trustees declaring academic standards to be the prime factor in evaluating presidents, by establishing general rules, not case-by-case, ad hoc decisions which can erode academic standards, by involving faculty in developing and enforcing all rules that protect academic principles, by universities agreeing to maintain academic standards in athletics by achieving consensus about research principles, by seeking stable government support and recognizing the risks of commodification and profit-seeking ventures.

Only a short time ago, university presidents were proclaiming higher education to be the prime growth industry of twenty-first century (see writings of Arthur Levine, former President, Columbia University's Teachers College). The current economic recession has slowed that kind of optimistic projection but not the super-charged advertising booster lingo of the "corporate" chief executive officer model of university president (see remarks of David Sexton, president of New York University). Yet the relations between industry/business and universities are troubled. Recent discussion in the United Kingdom on intellectual property is pertinent.

Business and industry argue that universities tend to overvalue their intellectual property. They say institutions do not account for the cost of taking technology to market, which makes it too expensive for business to work with them to exploit it. Universities claim that business takes advantage of them. Companies see higher education as a cheap source of research and which often pays the full economic costs since the laboratories are state-funded. So institutions are anxious to hold on to intellectual property rights (see *London Times Higher Education Supplement*, June 13, 2003).

Bok's hope seems to be contradicted by this new breed of university president who speaks ever glowingly of establishing a new paradigm for the American university "by building" the "brand name" to generate "a high volume buzz by recruiting the celebrity, golden boy" type of professor.

The slogan for building the brand is to create "the world's first global university in the world's truly global city—the epicenter—of the world's epicenter—New York City. The emphasis is to be on the "Common Enterprise" as an elaborate marketing strategy (see *New York Times Magazine*, June 8, 2003, pp. 72–76).

Of course, such globalization may require more precise definition than it now receives. It is uneven in scope in that academic research proceeds further in science than in humanities. Science and engineering demand global commonality, communicability and contemporaneity while the humanities and social science stress analysis in diverse and unique cultures, i.e. globalization operates in science and engineering and internationalization in humanities and social sciences. The question arises as to whether productivity has improved at a rate commensurate with investment in globalization and internationalization of higher education.

Turning to the category of diversity, one recognizes that the benefits of diversity in higher education culturally and socially are inestimable. Yet the flip side of this development must be made transparent in order to cope with the increasing complex consequences of diversity. The growth in new types of students is being accompanied by an increase in the numbers of reluctant students, and of "general" students without a strong subject commitment. More students lack the requisite basic academic ability with remedial education being increasingly needed.

The curriculum becomes more chaotic as the university becomes more diverse and inclusive of different instrumental needs, resulting in a state of anomie for higher education. Failure to articulate smoothly the connection between general education curriculum, primitive development of systematic research on curriculum lack of interest by society at large in university education are vulnerabilities in the diversification process. Other weaknesses are the "disconnect" between the first two and last two years of bachelor degree education, difficulty in equating the first two years of a four year college and the two years of community college curricula in quality and scope.

For the most part, a lag remains between the state of educational methods and faculty development and their reformation necessary for basic higher education reforms in process.

Yet it is important to remember, as Clark Kerr has asserted, change influenced by market are accepted in a way that reforms originating in concerns for educational policy are not. The appropriate emblem, to Kerr, for the American college might be the traditional open book, but lying on a sales counter.

He points to one heralded reform that failed—general education—which was supplanted by the fundamental shift from liberal to vocational studies and within vocational studies from one field to another—with engineering, for example, changing back and forth in attractiveness to students.

Other critics in confronting pressure for reform have conceptualized differently. Richard Rorty writes that the role of higher education, unlike that provided in the schools, is no longer to incorporate given truths but to stimulate the imagination and critical mind, to fuel doubts about unquestioned truths and the consensus of predominant prejudices. To simplify, schools produce literate citizens and universities produce creative individuals. Jean-Jacques Paul believes universities were built upon different layers of sedimental knowledge, upon partial adaptation to successive environmental changes. They have to preserve functions such as promoting general and theoretical knowledge and encouraging reflective and critical thinking. Pushed too hard, reforms may damage these beneficial effects.

The challenge is to modify the cost of the six identified reforms, which are in process in the university world. For the link to industry the cost may be decline in teaching quality. For the increase in private funding it may be loss of autonomy. For globalizing economic development the price to be paid may be loss in local, regional, national pride and incentive. For diversification it may be limiting policy and research progress; for government and political influence, the expense may decline in meritocracy. Adverse consequences can carry over into research. Some leading research groups feel they must undertake research that is conceptualized as acceptable to policy makers whose views are anticipated carefully by research councils. Appointments might be made in deference to, or even likely to be favored in, the market place of sponsorship rather than by strict ordering of academic merits of applicants.

The former president of Stanford University, Donald Kennedy, has also placed caution signs on the highway to reforms. The question arises as to whether the merging of academic work with practice, and the pursuit of knowledge for its own sake with market demands affect standards of the academic enterprise. Does the rise of the inter-disciplinary or trans-disciplinary harm the research and creation benefits of the discipline?

For any change or reform, governance, in Kennedy's view, is absolutely critical, i.e. governance defined as organization, as context that directs how choices are made and who makes them.

These are numerous illustrations of adverse results of some measures for reforms. Dependence on government funding results in efforts to restrict access of foreign nationals not only to data but to academic seminars, to limit freedom of scholarly publications, to government's censoring of faculty member statements requiring universities to justify research costs in the same manner as those "for-profit" defense procurement sectors at great institutional cost. These are all substantial consequences to dependence on government funding.

Another warning sign for reform is that a "cognition map" of universities exists, that is, not all universities are or should be the same. Professional training has been rethought and reorganized much more regularly and systematically than training in the humanities and sciences. The disciplinary structure of universities comes up against the fact that the world's problems do not conform to that structure. Moreover, the impact of the clash of the subculture of traditional university and the subculture of post-modernism is not yet clear.

In addition, the ramifications of Stephen Stigler's landmark essay on competition within universities on major, higher education reforms have not been fully worked out even though it has been a decade since he concluded that faculty own the university and competition among and within universities is a competition among faculties.

Faculty act as if they own their universities even if active ownership is constrained by rules imposed by trustees and government and vested in academic administrators who may serve at the pleasure of the faculty in fact, if not in name.

The intellectual competition is among peers at the universities. The competition for resources is within and between universities. Expanding electronic networks eventually leads to weakening of institution identity, the cost of information technology progress.

Stigler insists that the greatest source of wisdom for reshaping the university's own programs and enacting reforms is its faculty. The growth of specialization has meant that only the faculty collectively is sufficiently knowledgeable to decide on major issues. By their intimate involvement within intellectual competition inside their discipline, faculty is aware of their strengths and shortcomings.

Institutions depend upon scholarly administrators and action depends on faculty's perception of the university's specific intellectual goals. Long discussion among faculty provides stable environment for sudden exploration into unknown intellectual territory.

Faculty thus can constitute a countervailing force to earmarking government funds under political pressure without any peer review, to agencies steering toward bolstering their own priorities in the setting of research agendas, to government emphasis on large-scale projects and research centers and centrally determined project and to benefits being diffused by broad-based funding of individual research projects.

Higher education reforms must also confront the policy that research agendas are increasingly set by government agency heads, program officers, congressional staff, advisory committees rather than by a wide network of young and energetic referees or faculty organization.

Intellectual competition among faculties of universities is fundamental to their success and to the completion of reforms and whatever diminishes their competition diminishes their institution and the possibilities of success for their higher education reforms.

The future strength and accomplishment, like their present strength and accomplishment, will be the product of the competition that organizes their activities. The ongoing and suggested reforms with respect to diversity, industry, government, privatization, globalization and finance are relevant responses to society's needs, but their success may depend on nature of governance, competition and the "cognition map" of universities, as well as on complete awareness of loss in certain academic values resulting from enactment of agreed-upon and socially and financially necessary reforms in higher education.

Chapter Ten

Legitimacy Crisis in Higher Education

Henry Wasser

The guild model of the university is still occasionally cited in the light of the current dominant entrepreneurial university. The crucible of the modern university contains the tangled thread of the "sixties" concept that challenged the so-called traditional universities in the marketplace of free ideas. That era demonstrated that free ideas do not occur in a competitive market place from which the best ideas emerge but more likely represent an arena for a power struggle over strongly held traditional beliefs, the sixties struggle reflected changing admissions policies that recognized both merit and past discrimination.

The meritocracy that emerged from the universities of the sixties enabled a talented generation to found the new knowledge society, that is, to recognize and realize the technological innovations of the Second World War, the electronic revolution.

Today's corporate model is no longer the industrial model of the implicit labor contract. A new ruthlessness characterizes the new economy. Management is becoming more and more autonomous, and it is this new model with which universities have to contend. If students are indeed customers, as much of the recent literature states, then they are being short-changed. If it is the celebrity professors who attract students to the university, shouldn't they demand their money back when graduate students and adjuncts teach them?

If to the ancient Greeks, the "arête" of a soldier is his bravery and the "arête" of an Athenian is his citizenship, is not the "arête" of the university the disinterested pursuit of knowledge? Its very success in the present generation attests its viability. To achieve recognition of the fact is its validation.

A legitimacy crisis exists in higher education.

There are numerous factors that lie behind this conclusion.

The following items are culled almost at random.

Knowledge is increasingly conceived of as a commodity, i.e. a stock rather than a process or flow.

Money from benefactors entails onerous conditions. In Canada, the Rotman Foundation's 15 million to the University of Toronto's business school appears to usurp a commitment to academic freedom. The business school promises to meet 26 pages of criteria including "ongoing support demonstrated by the members of the faculty." The Foundation has the power to stop the money, which is being parceled out until 2011. As private sector donations, often rewarded by the naming of schools for the benefactor, begin to replace government funding, research priorities may be altered. One-fifth of 55 business faculties in Canadian universities have either coupled or completely replaced the names of their institution with that of a successful businessman-donor. Most top-ranking business schools in American universities have given themselves names that help develop an identity independent from their university (e.g. Wharton/Pennsylvania, Kellogg/Northwester, Sloan/M.I.T., Fuqua/Duke, Simon/Rochester, et al.

The University of Central London will teach and train its academic staff to woo and win commercial business. Courses are offered in business skills, negotiation, bidding and presentation to tempt academics to venture together into the commercial world and to develop the core skills people need to go into business, speak the language, get involved in commercially driven projects and to have the opportunity to attract people from the business world to their faculties.

George Washington University has established a College of Professional Studies where the Dean is also the Chief Executive Officer of the George Washington Solution, a new for-profit subsidiary of the university.

Tenure has been weakened, as universities become more ame more business enterprises and corporate-like, viewing faculty as employees. A Boston University Provost declares, "Can tenure be justified in an era when colleges and universities have taken on so many characteristics of business enterprise?" A higher-education consultant asserts that faculty still have a lot of old-time Renaissance rules, including tenure and most see themselves as free agents." He says, "But they are operating in a modern, corporate setting where tuition is now $1,000 a week, and colleges and universities have been forced to become more corporate-like in the way they operate." A literature scholar echoes these comments. "There is some kind of shift going on whereby university faculty are seen less as independent contractors than as employees." A former S.U.N.Y. Chancellor justifies the trend. "There is a far greater range of productivity in the profession than in almost any other. I think faculty have gotten used to free time as a right and I think it has gotten out of hand."

On-line growth has meant for one that the divorce of intellectual capital from the actual content of teaching and learning threatens everything that is valuable in the American higher education system. Over time, the separation of curricular planning from actual teaching will discourage talented faculty, replicating in the academy the same problems of finding effective teachers that we already confront in our schools. Since the trend in higher education is toward scripted lessons, the new for-profit, on-line plans for higher learning are built into one-size-fits-all models with "expert faculty" creating courses complete with lesson plan and script. "Contract course managers" are then listed to actually "teach" the students script in hand.

The potential for commercial rewards colors researchers' judgment to lure them away from important research that does not yield a lucrative patent, spin-off in stock options in the company sponsoring the work. Ironically, the university is often a corporate entity that denies its corporate nature. There is no longer a sense of shared purpose in Cardinal Newman's "familiar inter-course." The purpose of corporate bottom-lining will produce a new kind of marginalism that seduces the most talented undergraduates who will no longer see people as multiple individuals but as globalized entities. It regards faculty as employees to be pressured into increasing productivity by teaching more and larger classes, at less pay, financing their own programs with out-side grant money, and trying to satisfy students as paying customers. Tenure is seen as impeding administrative and management flexibility; merit pay be-comes market pay. The rhetoric of collegiality becomes a smoke screen for corporate authority.

Instancing higher education as a commercial product are the proposals be-fore the World Trade Organization to make importing and exporting of higher education subject to the complex rules of WTO protocols, which mainly re-move restrictions designed to ensure quality and to maintain national control over higher education. If higher education is regarded as a "service" as the United States has proposed to the WTO, then all regulatory mechanisms could be deemed illegal in the name of the free market.

The underlying concept is knowledge as an economic instrument rather than for moral character or responsible citizenship or culture, or for its own sake. The premise is that students know their needs or that governments do and that needs are always to be defined in the form of skills and preferences. Govern-ments use fiscal policy to drive institutions to market and consequently to con-trol both markets and universities (France, UK). But as Lord Annan asserts, all

policies must at bottom understand the struggle to know something, "to produce out of the chaos of the human experience some grain of order won by the
intellect."

The onslaught continues. A recent report at the Center for Science in the
Public Interest, approved by 35 university and business leaders does not accept the view that universities are becoming research and development arms
of companies. Nonetheless, company sponsored research has risen from 9%
(2 billion dollars) of university research in 1998 to 9.4% (2.2 billion dollars) in 1999. The report urges universities to adopt hiring, tenure and promotion policies that reward researchers for collaborating with industries
and is concerned more with fostering university corporate relations than
with creating an educational environment where robust science is conducted. The Association of Governing Boards of universities in 1998
shifted markedly from traditional and generally accepted policy on shared
governance, which had recommended a strong role for professors in both
selecting and evaluating presidents, to advocating centralization of authority with a role for faculty and other "stakeholders" only as outlined by governing boards.

Universities locate for-profit companies that market courses delivered on
the Internet and seeks corporate partners to develop innovations for deliver-
ing courses online. Multi-media company Knowledge University has a 20%
share in Vacet; a commercial distance education company established by six
universities in the USA and UK, NYU and University of Maryland, in particular.

Columbia University forms a for-profit online partnership with other institutions to exploit new media technology. A critic notes that the new technologies require re-institutionalizing of the university as a more corporate
kind of organization where goals, roles, identities, rules, and operating procedures are made more explicit than those of the collegial model absorbing
them (THES 7/30/1999).

In Canada, a growing proportion of federally funded university-based research comes with a requirement that projects have a corporate partner. The
President of the Canadian Association of University Teachers comments,
"Turning scholars into entrepreneurs undercuts the very idea of post-secondary education since the job of entrepreneur, urged on academia by government and business, is to develop and sell a product, not to pursue truth.

New managerial cultures derived from a corporate atmosphere may have
been grafted on in a piecemeal fashion to existing structures, and since this
has happened in universities, professional and professorial power is being in-
crementally diluted and displaced by ideological new managerial reforms
(Rosemary Deem , THES).

Jeremiads have more relevance than ever. As one scholar points out, the liberal arts nourish and open hearts and minds through dialogue and debate. They deepen a democratic citizenship and leadership that, in the past, faced humanity's struggles toward justice, honor, and freed of choice, but in the present atmosphere feel the pressure of corporate bottom-lining—a new kind of managerialism that often ignores mankind's tribulations. Or, as AAUP's director of research notes: the profession has changed for the worse. Universities now rely heavily on part-time and non-tenured instructors and faculty members are stretched in more directions. "The philosophy now is that students are our customers." The AAUP (American Association of University Professors) must continue to battle a creeping decline in the quality of higher education, he says, comparing what he sees as a lack of investment in higher education with what happens to a chocolate bar when the price of cocoa rises: "You put more milk and sugar in to compensate and eventually your milk chocolate is just milk. You can gradually decline and no one notices."

Ortega y Gassett's decision remains ever relevant—the life of the people needs to have the university participate as university in its affairs rather than as a corporate entrepreneurial organization. Confronting current conditions in society requires a complex, historical sense of the values inherent in the university, presently coping with an entrepreneurial emphasis. This sense of values can be strengthened by assuming the outlook and tactic suggested by Bjørn Wittrock who writes that even in an age dominated by applied science and technology or in a time when the impossibility of communication is assented to by linguistic, philosophic, and literary critics, science, knowledge and learning still manage to open cultural gates. The problem of the universality of the university does not fade because of emphasis on the particular. Universality is the "real" problem and the "real" concern. To deal with it, he concludes, we shall have to think and act as if, despite market, political, and social pressures, we were freely communicating colleagues in a university that reformers have envisioned but never fully realized.

Chapter Eleven

Universities and the Corporate Model

Henry Wasser

In a study several years ago, I noted that questionnaire information gathered from European and American university heads led to the conclusion that the particular discipline of the leader of an institution of higher education could suggest the social value attached by society to that institution and that comparison with another society could highlight different aspects of social value and esteem. Comparing results from European and American university heads made it clear that Europe's choices were more heavily from engineering, biology, medicine and physical sciences whereas America favored education, humanities, fine arts, or theology with roughly the same percentage as in Europe from the social sciences. This, however, was mainly a shift from one kind of disciplinary training to another—which might be reflected in leadership style.

But the change in the last decade has been seismic in scope. The corporate image dominates the universities. Business, computer science, productivity, strategy, systems analysis, information technology are the background for university leaders, except where gender and affirmative action may determine selection. Political acumen, experience and allegiance and budget analysis are currently the preferred qualifications, especially for public university presidents.

This corporate model has brought about an executive pay category with a corps of vice presidents, a title not previously known in the academic universe, along with officers and directors for human resources, development and information technology.

Then there is the wholesale adoption of the language of the marketplace—entrepreneurial, enterprise university, characterization of higher education as the great growth industry of the 21st century, cost benefit analysis, spinoff "for profit" companies from universities, productivity, credential training by and for regional companies, assessment, performance indicators—the language is of the corporate, not university community.

The current domination of the university by administrators and managers and the belief that the central figure of the university is no longer the professor who is both scholar and teacher but the executive vice chancellor or senior vice president to whom both apparatchiks and professors are answerable describes (see Bill Reading's University in Ruins, Harvard University Press, 1996) a university far different from that envisioned by the venerable humanist and provost Jacques Barzun in 1968. The enlightened and liberal administrator from the professorial ranks was to be the hero of the story of the university. Barzun proposed the formation of an autonomous stratum of nonacademic administrators within the university as a "second layer."

"If caught young, such men [sic] can become top civil servants and be accepted as professionals without being scholars; they can enjoy a prestige of their own and share fully in the amenities that are widely believed to adorn campus life; and they can do more than any other agency to render efficient the workings of the great machine" (p. 191).

Similarly, for a considerable length of time it was thought the administrative necessities of the university could best be met by training the professors, not by creating a class of managers—in this way the values and traditions of the university would be more or less retained while still meeting the needs of society.

What has happened is distinctly different although it could have been anticipated. The new class took over authority and power at the expense of collegiality.

Even curricula and programs, formerly the domain solely of the professor were taken over by the manager/administrator and the trustees, especially in public universities. Humanities can now be taught in a cybernetic universe subject often to the authority of the information technology expert.

Yet it was only a few years ago that traditional scholars were decrying the effect of government actions and policies on higher education in the twentieth century.

They believed such policies undercut the role of the scholar as critical thinker, influenced the acceptance of vocational goals for higher education, promoted the role of universities and scholars/researchers as managers of human resources and reinforced the certifying role of universities and colleges by increasing access to youth cohort groups.

They did not foresee rapid encroachment and the dominant 21st century role of trustees appointed as political henchmen of elected political figures, especially state governors. The marketing role became the informing principle for politics and for these trustees. A sitting SUNY president has courageously written that for such boards capital reigns supreme, and success is measured in net income and levels of productivity.

"The spread," he continues, "of this ideology has turned university presidents into chief executive officers, provost into chief operating officials. Deans have become middle management and department chairs lower level management. Faculty members are not labor and students are consumers or clients. Assessment and accountability refer to measuring productivity; colleges and universities set up entrepreneurial ventures and seek presidents from outside higher education.

A random selection of titles within universities and from advertised vacancies attest to the corporatization of higher education:

- Director of Office of Intellectual Property and Technology Transfer
- Director of Marketing and Communication
- Vice President of Human Resources
- Chief Operating Officer
- Director of Compliance and Education
- Director of Office of Integrated Risk Management
- Vice President for Marketing
- Campus Executive Officer (CEO)/Vice Provost
- Director of Academic Personnel
- Associate Director of Service Learning
- Entrepreneurship Learning Director
- Head of Academic Development
- Head of Learning and Information Services
- Marketing/Public Relations Manager
- Senior Director of Corporate Relations

Looking at the advertisements, we note that the technology transfer and intellectual property specialist is to develop a patenting and licensing strategy and focus on marketing such; the Director of Compliance and Education is to develop research related education programs to address the needs of the community; the Chief Operating Officer is to develop strategy for growth and excellence along with administering various schools within the university.

The business/corporate titles and discourse carry over into recruitment of students. A group of 28 college presidents invites high-price, brand-name private institutions to eliminate price competition by private collective action.

Private colleges compete for students in the same ways and for the same reasons that producers of other goods and services compete for customers.

Selling a college education is considered a business and competition for the most coveted students grows keener every day.

The strategy behind colleges' financial aid to students is not different from the rebates and low-cost financing that automobile manufacturers offer to make their products more attractive.

Private high-price, high-prestige colleges want to avoid price competition because that is in their own best interests. These colleges, like businesses who would limit or eliminate price competition, claim to be doing so in the best interest of consumers and the public, not admitting that the motive is the self-same business primary interest.

Even the august American Association of University Professors advertises that market place academics face liability risks in the academic arena previously associated only with the business world. Such risks arise from claims associated with dismissal, suspension disciplinary action, student evaluations judgments relating to salary, promotion, rank, leave of absence, publishing of research papers, etc. Contending that the liability your university provides you is insufficient, A.A.U.P. suggests purchasing liability protection.

A former head of American Council of Learned Societies complains that college and university presidents are cheerleaders for commercialization, believing that if universities do not proceed, the window of opportunity will close as proprietary institutions take over digital distance education.

Trustees endeavoring to recoup the enormous cost of digitalization, equipment purchase, maintenance and retention of high-price, high-tech empoloyees will turn to for-profit alliances or create their own entities such as Fathom: Columbia, London School of Economies, and other universities.

Stanley Katz declares that action has already begun with respect to intellectual property, to move informational technology into educational perspective, creating a chief information officer (CIO) to cope with the new technology and concludes that it is essential to create authority structures that evaluate technology needs and opportunities in terms of intellectual and educational priorities rather than administrative procedures.

But in research fear is spreading about the growth of corporate influence at universities. A celebrated instance is the 25 million dollar strategic alliance between the plant biology department of the University of California at Berkeley and a multi-national life-sciences company based in Switzerland, detailed in an Atlantic Monthly article on corporate intrusion in academe called "The Kept University." The respected *Nature* periodical in an editorial questions whether the university-industry complex is out of control. The A.A. U. P. warns that the arrangements like the Berkeley-Novartis could distort students' priorities and compromise scientific openness.

For $5 million dollars a year Novartis gets first look at virtually all of the research of plant and microbiologists along with first rights to license a share of what they invent and can review doctoral dissertations before they are published. Yet Novartis also profits from an academic research establishment built largely with public money.

Not just title but the language of discourse echoes the corporatization of the university. One college president speaks of higher education as the leading growth industry of the twenty-first century. A critic writes education is the oil of the twenty-first century—"we are sitting on the reserves." Higher education, another notes, is a 228 billion dollar enterprise.

Online institutions like University of Phoenix, DeVry Institute, Motorola University are gaining legitimacy, blurring the distinction between propri-etary and non-profit institutions.

They, with a small number of academic celebrities, a larger number of learning facilitators, create and administer "learning ware products" for an ar-ray of for-profit service companies who in turn sell their products to students.

Such organizations are hardly a community of scholars but more like a drug company that has work-for-hire knowledge workers producing propri-etary research.

Online companies trade on the prestige of great academic names, bear de-velopment costs while the institutions gets a small piece of the company and a mere fraction of the gross receipts. Once a university permits itself to be sub-sumed into its brand name, it becomes a "production house for making knowl-edge products," a further development of its present patenting and licensing ac-tivities. The political model of the late 20th century has apparently been superseded by the 21st century model of managerial professionalism.

The American trinity of teaching, research and service (to the community), which superseded the European trinity of teaching ,research and learning, is now being replaced by teaching, research and business, industry, online service.

Any casual survey reveals the overwhelming extent to which corporativism has taken over structure, content, professionalizing and discourse in the uni-versities. We have been familiar with the long-standing character-building university of Cardina Newman or the research university of Humboldt or the liberal arts small college or the pursuit of knowledge for truth and for its own sake, of elements in major universities. But all of these goals have been in-creasingly under attack in the interests of instrumentalism, community de-mands of political intrusion if not domination. The time-honored institution, however, has found it necessary increasingly to compromise with such oppo-sition to values, traditional or not.

But the pervasive current activity of the on-line, virtual universities, cre-ated by corporations, increased political interference to the point of legislators and governors becoming change-agents, control of substantial research, applied or basic, by such entities as global pharmaceutical companies, brings in their wake treatment of faculty as employees, students as customers, trustees as board of directors, administrators as chief executive and chief operating officers leading ultimately to the elimination of faculty tenure, large-scale employment of adjuncts and part-timers, making a race of shared governance, and a fact of dominant instrumentalizing of curriculum and programs—so much so that characterizations like ruin of the university no longer seem hysterical. Ominous also is the increasing emphasis on productivity of faculty by several well-known administrators and university presidents, strongly backed by trustees and politicians.

How does one measure productivity of a professor—quantity of publications, hours spent in the class, profitability of research, number of citations? Can you really compare productivity of faculty with that of the high-tech employee of a tele-communications corporation? Or a tire builder in the rubber industry?

Such comparisons may seem far-fetched, but the intent of applying a most significant term of corporate activity to faculty is clear: to restrain the independence and freedom of the professor by holding him to non-academic standards.

And where in all this is the interplay of ideas, pursuit of knowledge for truth and for its own sake that we had come to expect from universities?

Chapter Twelve

The Growth of Short-Cycle Higher Education

Henry Wasser

I

The strengthening of short-cycle higher education, whether Fachhochschule, university college, I.U.T, regional college, H.B.O. or polytechnic has been a fact of tertiary education for the last thirty years and has been an appropriate response to three different factors: economic, social and financial.

From the economic and labor-market point of view, the non-university sector was needed to furnish the labor force with graduates in the fields of engineering and commerce, who could function at the middle levels. From a social standpoint, developing short or practice-oriented courses outside the universities was thought to provide higher education opportunities for a majority of secondary school graduates. And, last, financing constraints on public budgets called for a decrease in public expenditure per graduate in higher education. The non-university sector was a way to achieve this.

A case in point is the Dutch H.B.O.'s, which established changes and prefigured proposals in other countries. External influence resulted from their achievement in gaining substantial power when they were entrusted by the government with stimulating and coordinating the process of merger between non-university institutions of higher education.

While the H.B.O.'s conducted first phase professional courses, universities offered the second phase, thus altering the previous circumstance wherein universities considered an H.B.O. degree as equivalent to one or two years of study. H.B.O.'s also decided which other non-university institutions could join the two-phase professional process.

While universities are governed by the academic community or academic administrators linked to them, non-university level institutions of higher education are guided by trustees or councils comprised of a majority of external representatives. An apparent consequence of this difference is that the range of potential innovation regarding studies is thought to be greater in H.B.O.'s.

A comparable attempt to individualize the mission and status of non-university tertiary education has been vigorously pursued in Norway where it was believed that novelty, experimental curricula, and imaginative faculty attracted students to district or regional colleges, which constituted a cultural counterweight to the force of national universities. Problem-oriented curricula organized cooperatively supplanted teacher-student authority relationships. District college innovations were considered to have resulted in increasing flexibility in the universities' handling of their problems.

Indeed, recently in Israel, where universities have been totally dominant, non-university higher education is developing with similar influences. While the best students go to the universities for medicine and law, the next level go to the newly established regional colleges since they offer fields of study that lead to good jobs in computer science and bio-technology. The least qualified may end up in the universities in such departments as physics and literature, for they are not popular at present and competition for admission to them is much less intense than it is in such subjects as business, computer science, economics and law.

At the onset of expansion, the picture was different. An invidious distinction was made between "noble" institutions (universities) and "less noble" ones (short-cycles in which the measure of the distinction was the traditional academic value system: theoretical and certain professional studies were in favorable contrast to more applicable professional and semi-professional knowledge and skills.

Parity of esteem with universities was seldom achieved; even the effort boomeranged, for it involved neglect of traditional short-cycle functions, which troubled prospective employers. What was apparent was that the closer the social distance between university and non-university higher education, the greater the concern over parity of esteem and over "identity."

The question arose early as to whether to strive for upgrading and risk becoming weak or second-choice university-type institutions or professional schools or to develop a different orientation emphasizing variety rather than quality.

In those early years of the '70s and '80s, distinguishing between models in the variety of tertiary education was necessary. There was the *binary model* (characteristic then of the United Kingdom and current in Germany). The *multi-purpose model* described Norway's district or regional college-university network curricula that enabled students to pass from one sector to another while maintaining the specific mission of both. The comprehensive model integrated short and long cycle higher education within an overall administrative body; examples were the Gesamthochschule such as Kassel in Germany and City University of New York in the U.S.A.

A different approach postulated an *integrated model* in which students with different prerequisites and abilities were admitted to the same institution and same course of studies as in the Swedish system, and a *diversified model* constituting a multitude of separate institutions within tertiary education as in the California three-tiered public higher-education or the State University of New York, the largest system in the U.S.A.

Two kinds of drift in short-cycle higher education were noted early—*academic drift* in which the tendency is to converge upon the university as the perceived ideal and *systemic drift*, the phenomenon wherein external pressures and norms begin to take the place of internal cultural values and norms inside the academic community.

II

Non-university institutions confront the problem of harmonizing vocationalism and education for competence with liberal education for personal development, as well as the problem of gaining acceptance for this compatibility in a policy environment which stresses the relevance of what is taught to the work place.

Universities face the dilemma of whether their charge includes training and education for the less esteemed professional and semi-professional technologies and of whether the inclusion of directly middle-job curricula within their precincts inevitably dilutes their traditional roles of basic research and knowledge dissemination and creation.

Arguments on both sides of the issue have been widely published. Among justifications for the independence of short-cycle institutions have been the notion that vocational post-secondary education produces new types of qualified manpower as well as an inter-disciplinary approach in place of the narrowly vocational oriented education of the schools. Moreover, short-cycle institutions provide some basic university education, which relieves universities of part of their teaching load, viz. in the instruction of first-year university courses. They are also more effective vehicles for continuing and adult education, which serve local needs for qualified manpower in areas where universities are distant or not interested in such a commitment. In addition, short-cycle institutions in contrast to universities are regionally relevant in accumulating and developing local applied research. Practice is added to theory or concept in the assumption that technical and para-professional programs at the secondary level have been upgraded to post-secondary status; a slowdown in social mobility has produced this upgrade in order to increase social movement. Regional boosterism and greater government control have also influenced this change.

An example of a country coming late to non-university higher education is Austria, which, aware of what worked and what did not work in the twenty-five year history of Fachhochschulen in neighboring Germany, proposed to transmit a high level of vocational-technical education to be capped by a Magister and Diplom-Ingenieur degree distinguished from university degrees by having F.H. added. Learning from still other countries, Austria legislated that applications for federal support to establish Fachhochschulen (F.H.'s) had to follow certain criteria, among them the innovative character of the program in terms of organization and content, the complementary nature of the program given existing institutions operating in the same or related fields, the prospects of viable, long-term development, the reduction of regional disparities within Austria in terms of access to institutions of higher education, the adaptation and use of existing resources such as physical plants, the participation of the private sector in financing, international exchange of students and teachers and the identification of new educational "target groups," e.g. apprentices, continuing education for employed adults (1993).

At the same time as Austria was enthusiastically entering non-university higher education, a noted policy analyst was cautioning that simply structured systems (Sweden in the last two decades, Italy) were having great difficulty in coping with the growing complexity of tasks. With some disdain he goes on to write that national public universities were turned into conglomerates within which an expanding number of interest groups fight all the battles involved "in doing everything for everyone." An informal agreement is reached about what the traditional university cannot do—does not want to do about short-cycle higher education and consequently creates or sees evolved institutes of technology and two-year colleges and other unites that award first degrees of their own. Moreover, the university cannot do—does not want to do extensive adult or continuing education, allowing "user-friendly" regional colleges to be established.

Consequently, sectorization, individualized by country, is seen as the answer to overloading simple structures. If additional types of institutions are not created or permitted to emerge, these all-in-one conglomerates become nominal forms and pretend to an academic unity that is artificial and asserted for political reasons (see Burton Clark, "The Problem of Complexity in Higher Education, pp. 266–267 in Sheldon Rothblatt and Bjorn Wittrock, *The European and American Universities Since 1800* (Cambridge University Press 1993).

Here, of course, all things "old and new" are measured by the rod of the traditional or perhaps more exactly the research university. The development of the comprehensive university, the Gesamthochschule, the integrated university, the Fachhochschule, the högskola, the polytechnic, in response to perceived social needs, are of lesser concern. The true agent for the great tasks of research and education is the university. The agent for the more trivial tasks of training and technological competence, semi-professional education and continuing, recurrent education is the short-cycle institutions which the universities permit to evolve sometimes within the public university, but better outside of it.

This analysis may well comfort the academic community as we have known it, but for our purpose it serves mainly to indicate that there are policy analysts who would have short-cycle structures exist outside the university since "within" they simply clutter or slow up or dilute traditional university functions.

And yet, it is clear that such institutions play different roles in different countries. Several studies have shown that the proportion of new higher education entrants into short-cycle institutions varied in the mid-eighties from 3–4% in Italy to more than 70% in Norway and Sweden (O.E.C.D. 1983, Clark 1985, Teichler 1988). Teichler has reminded us that there is no generally agreed upon delineation between university and non-university higher education among European countries. In some, he has argued, a "vocational emphasis of non-university higher education was considered to differ only moderately from university education. In others, a vocational profile was thought to contrast sharply from that of the universities. It has even been observed that the differences have gradually blurred over the years as a result of "academic drift" in non-university higher education and "vocational drift" in the university sector.

A more recent O.E.C.D. study (1991) confirms differences in size and therefore in importance. The ratio of entry—university and non-university— into full-time tertiary education it shows may be divided into three groupings: university dominating U.S. 38/32, Finland 32/26, France 26/16, Denmark 25/10, Australia 32/18, Germany (West) 32/11, United Kingdom 17/9, Austria 20/6, Czech and Slovak Republic 13/1, Turkey 10/1. A middle category has the ration roughly even with Switzerland 11/10, Belgium 21/21, Japan 23/27, Ireland 17/13, Portugal 19/14. The third group shows weighting toward non-university higher education: Sweden 11/34, the Netherlands 11/26 and Hungary 4/8.

Since it has been frequently said that the German Fachhochschule has been among the most successful of non-university higher education institutions, a brief description here will be useful.

In 1971 former vocational schools were upgraded to Fachhochschulen. Employers' representatives at first opposed their establishment, contending that the consequence would be blocking the road to advanced vocational training for talented workers and having a too-theoretical approach in the upgraded institutions. However, they came to support FH's strongly when they saw a loss of youth to the universities. Indeed, they also opposed the "third" way, Gesamthochschule (the comprehensive university), preferring the twin tracks of "theoretical" in the universities and vocational/practical in the Fachhochschulen.

There were other opponents who, although a small minority, vigorously attacked the increase in number of shorter courses because criteria were not defined by which courses should be allocated between universities and FH's but were selected as the least expensive of reform solutions, thereby highlighting the prestige status of universities. They also found a failure to improve quality teaching, a stated objective of FH's, and the distinction between developmental research (FH) and fundamental research (universities) to be artificial. The conclusion to their argument was to propose a new type of tertiary education structure—the mass university which would integrate the FH's within the university/system and have a broad range of differentiated courses that are thought most fit to meet the challenge of a changing society (see Jürgen Schramm, unpublished Ms. "The Impact of Unification on the System of Higher Education of the Federal Republic of Germany and the Special Case of Universities in Berlin").

Fachhochschulen spokesmen are presently waging the fight on a different front. In order to market themselves internationally, FH's want to be called universities (perhaps universities of applied studies and research). Their academic leaders are certain that their degrees are more than equal to international bachelor degrees. Moreover, they want the right to award international bachelor of arts degrees after six semesters of instruction on the way to diplomas, which are awarded after a minimum of eight semesters. The university degree requires a minimum of ten semesters. The strongest subjects in the Fachhochschulen are engineering, information technology, economics and business management. On the whole, Fachhochschulen appear to have gained by their separation within the higher education system and are looking for increase in status on their own right without being measured in traditional university terms (*Times Higher Educational Supplement* 1997).

The trajectory for Swedish short-cycle higher education has been different; Proponents hold that the most striking characteristic has been the integration of the general, vocational and further education within one national system without any clear-cut distinctions between the three functions. All units offered the same types of study programs and independent courses from the largest universities with their full range of faculties and programs to the smaller regional university colleges with only a small set of study programs and courses within one or two program sectors and thus different from countries with binary systems divided between academic and vocational.

Yet like binary systems, in Sweden permanent pure research organizations and such institutes as medicine along with graduate programs for doctoral studies are only in universities. But mainly, there is integration of short-cycle higher education into a national system with localized or regionalized components—university colleges—rather than binary separation.

These developments occurred despite indifference from university leaders as evidenced in the Barcelona meeting of the European Rectors Conference (1993). They estimate that about one third of an age group attends an institution of higher learning resulting in "universitization of vocational schools" and "professionalization of universities" (Gilles Bertrand). In their view, the tertiary educational system has not fully adjusted to the new demands resulting from the greatly diversified social and educational background of today's student body. The tertiary educational system, in their opinion, has not fully adjusted to the new demands arising from the highly diversified social and educational background of [the] current student body. Its response has been mainly institutional or structural in upgrading vocational schools and technological institutes or polytechnics and downgrading the classical university.

Ralf Dahrendorf has asserted that Europe had not yet found the way to deal with mass higher education. The rectors apparently believe that an adequate solution to this problem must include saving the traditional European university and at the same time take account of the varied needs and abilities of the "new" students. This solution depends on a combination of further institutional diversification, carefully crafted study programs and individual student support policies. Efficiency would allow for individual career paths by increasing the system's vertical and horizontal permeability while individual student support should give relevant information for an intelligent choice between alternative career paths.

Stockholm University's rector noted the echoes of the German debate in which Fachhochschulen (university colleges in Sweden) have displayed more flexibility and efficiency in education and training than the traditional universities which are overcrowded and generally not capable of adjusting to new societal needs. He thought such allegations should stimulate the universities to reflect on their primary obligations towards society and to take a firm stand against those external demands that they simply were not meant to fulfill. The modern university, a very complex institution, serves many purposes simultaneously, producing internal tensions. But one common characteristic, he concludes, is the bond uniting research and education. From that Humboldtian stance, all courses are derived.

The Netherlands took a different and highly individual approach to short cycle higher education. Instead of separation and independence (Fachhochschule model) or national [system?] transformation of the entire higher education system into högskola (early Swedish model or the binary model based regionally with emphasis on semi-professional preparation (present Swedish model). The Dutch merged all short-cycle institutions into a national system of H.B.O.'s aside from the universities.

Sectors were then treated as collections of coherent subjects: Nine different sectors were distinguished: Arts, Science, Law, Economics, Health, Behavior and Society, Technology, Education, and Agriculture. All institutional policies were to be market-oriented; almost all courses and research were to be inter-disciplinary, with stress on internationalization and quality control.

Previously, H.B.O.'s had been uni-sectoral, now they were multi-sectoral, but their organizational structures resembled those of universities. These changes were brought about by strong government intervention for separate but equal systems. Moreover, these institutions discovered they had a comprehensive national planning system, which increased professional instead of institutional orientation. Steering or guidance at the sector, instead of at the institutional level, stimulated this tendency.

Therefore, separation or independence of short-cycle structures resulted. In the Dutch case, a national non-university higher-education system and increased professional orientation at the individual institution.

The American community college, generally at a lower level than European short-cycle higher education, can therefore be only casually compared. Actually, the American four-year technical college is more equivalent. It is, however, the argument for or against separation or independence from university that turns us to the community colleges, which are most often separate under independent coordinating boards. Even where previously controlled by or placed in a flagship university, change has come as in the state of Kentucky where the governor has succeeded in removing community colleges from the University of Kentucky, arguing that such separation leaves the University free to raise its research status and to increase the flexibility of the community to meet the training needs of regional economic development.

Arguments have tended rather to consider the increase in vocationalizing community colleges, the decline in curricula as preparation for transfer to universities. Seeking the origins of this change leads to several questions.

Did students demand or oppose occupational education? If the students did not demand vocationalization of short-cycle higher education, did business do so to secure publicly subsidized employee training to reduce its labor training costs?

Were community colleges established to protect the selectivity of the elite universities? Or were the community colleges established primarily by government officials in pursuit of public policy for social good?

This ideological debate assumed a separate short-cycle facility and concentrated on whose interests it served. The major structural debate was whether to overcome institutional separation between community and four-year colleges, either by transforming community colleges into four-year colleges, or by converting community colleges into two-year university branches.

Either change would probably improve transfer procedure — lower-division academic preparation would be better utilized because faculty in the lower and upper divisions would be the same. But it must be noted that 65% to 80% of community-college entrants are not baccalaureate aspirants but rather are looking for vocational, remedial, or adult recreational education.

A branch campus is likely to put less emphasis on vocational education. Some are entirely academic. Others maintain strong vocational programs. They may facilitate the pursuit of the baccalaureate degree by making transfer and admission easier. Similar transfers can be made with difficulty in the German system and are practically impossible in Greek higher education, where the state has decreed (1993) that for those who fail the general examination for the university, there is an alternative open: Institutions of Professional Knowledge.

Further, since students of the branch campuses are members of the university, they are more inclined than community-college students to transfer, receive financial aid, be prepared for upper division and be more compatible to the upper division college. Studies show that twice as many students transfer from the branch campuses than from independent community colleges.

The French experience, my final example, has been different. A policy analyst has recently remarked that with respect to I.U.T.'s — French short-cycle higher-education structures — very bright students opted for them because they were selective, but the teaching was not really intended for them, and they did not really want to be trained in technical subjects and did not envision a technical career. And when after two years they applied for transfer to universities, they discovered the two years were not at the cultural level of the university and the two years were, consequently, in a sense wasted. Others were opposed to universities devoting so much resources and time to short-cycle, short-term training (I.U.T.'s were both outside and within universities) and therefore slighting their major objective, which is scientific development and training by research for students of heterogeneous background. To avoid difficulty, there has to be cross-linked schemes and appropriate bridging courses.

My conclusion is not dramatic. Separation vs. integration with regard to short-cycle and university higher education turns out to have variations and modifications on both sides of the contrast, depending upon country. What seems clear is that the whole of higher or tertiary education continues to change and that its diverse structures, because of the rapid movement in higher education since the 1960's have not been fully formed or matured.

Chapter Thirteen

The European Community and Higher Education

Henry Wasser

Ladislav Cerych, senior advisor to TEMPUS, in writing about Western Europe in 1992 (1989 Cerych) has enumerated the significant areas in higher education for reference after 1992: curriculum, global and diversified system, institutional autonomy, responsibility, and responsiveness, competitiveness, equality of opportunity, continuing education, cooperation with industry, use of communication and information technologies, contribution to economic and social cohesion and to regional development and foreign language teaching and learning. He does not rank the items in this exhaustive enumeration. Although it would be useful for Western Europe and Community planning to establish priorities, it would be even more valuable to decide which of these areas should be dealt with now with respect to Central/East Europe. While TEMPUS has selected Poland, Hungary and Czechoslovakia as being sufficiently advanced for its program, and the Federal Republic of Germany partly under the aegis of the Community has a plan, apparently controversial in its mainly absorption approach for higher education in its eastern Länder, it is not clear what the immediate priorities are for Cerych's decalogue (Cerych, 1989).

Some changes were predictable, even automatic — the elimination of catechistical Marxian ideological curricula, the rise of business and management programs and the demand for "state of the art" communication and information technology. The call for global and diversified system, economic and social cohesion, even regional development is not opposed, it simply requires vast input of resources. Indeed Western and Southern European higher education in these matters is still in the process of evolution and elaboration. It is inevitable that English would replace Russian as the second language in universities in Central Europe. Cooperation with industry, highly developed in most of Europe, is in the beginning stages in Central/East Europe where privatization has only begun. Similarly, continuing education has generally meant recurrent education through a lifetime to prevent obsolescence and adult education for cultivation and joy of learning. Neither can have much meaning at present for Central/East Europe in that technological development has been mainly static, and little leisure time has been available in the subsistence existence of the East.

Institutional autonomy, responsibility and responsiveness to economic and societal needs are relative. The West debates government intervention in higher education, at present, loosening government intrusion at the expense of increasing accountability controlled by the government. Such argument, however, has not hitherto been possible in the previously highly government controlled universities of the East. Flexibility of the relationship is only now seen as possible. Response to social needs not so diverse as in the U.S. nevertheless appears in the West sensitive to market forces when compared to the previous highly bureaucratized central planning of the East.

Competitiveness among the universities in Western Europe is in motion, again slight compared to U.S. but significant compared to Eastern Europe. Examples are recent polls of attractiveness to students of German universities, the evolution of universities, and projects in government allocation of research budget in the United Kingdom. Mobility is substantially on the rise in the West, only commencing in the East and that with the aid of TEMPUS.

TEMPUS was designed, it is officially stated, in response to the needs in Central/Eastern Europe and is modeled upon but different from COMETT, ERASMUS, and LINGUA. It relates to activities at the level of higher education especially developing teaching capacities at universities and post-secondary institutions. These include various forms of education, training and retraining of teaching staff as well as relationships with partners external to education such as industrial and to business enterprises and the development of curriculum.

Eligible for financial support are plans for study at higher education institutions involving acquisition of knowledge and skills by various categories of students or adult learners seeking further training. The exception is youth exchange activities, which fall within the framework of TEMPUS even without a link to higher education.

The essential aims of TEMPUS are, of course, to promote quality and support the development and evolution of the higher education systems in the countries of Central/Eastern Europe, which are eligible for economic aid—Poland and Hungary in 1990–1991. TEMPUS will also be interested in a wide range of organizations, industrial as well as educational. The documents use the terms "industry" and "enterprise" to indicate all types of economic activity, public and local authorities, independent economic organizations, foundations and professional organizations.

The operating budget of the Trans European Mobility Programme for University Students (TEMPUS) was around 107,000,000 ECU's for 1990–1992 and limited to Poland, Hungary and Czechoslovakia. One expert observer has called it a species of high-powered son of ERASMUS using as a kind of model the Marshall Plan Aid Programme in its objective to reconstruct higher education and develop particular skills in management, economics and technology for Central/Eastern Europe (Neave, 1990).

A paradoxical circumstance that has arisen is that Central/Eastern Europe passionate for a market economy; a free enterprise system, is receiving most of its help for restructuring its higher education system from the European Community which remains basically a bureaucratic system even in its higher education efforts. And bureaucratic distinctions have consequences even in this most recent initiative. For example, while continuing education and re-training at higher education levels falls within the TEMPUS scheme, they are subject to certain limitations in view of the complementary activities covered by the European Training Foundation. Nevertheless continuing education subsidy will serve to bring central and eastern European university teachers fully up to date with the latest state of knowledge in their field, and financial support will be provided to the universities to enable them to introduce or improve their structural capacities in continuing education, especially with regard to cooperation with industry.

TEMPUS is actually to be coordinated by twenty-four Western nations. This "G24" group, apart from E.C. member states, includes the six EFTA countries and Turkey, U.S.A., Canada, Japan, Australia and New Zealand. They may be involved in various ways such as exchanging information, co-ordinating national initiatives with TEMPUS, co-financing, use of TEMPUS facilities and channeling bilaterally funded exchange actions.

It is held that Community funds may be used only for activities between E.C. member states and the eligible countries. They take the form and title of Joint European Projects, Mobility Grants for Staff and Students, and Complementary Activities.

Under Joint European Projects there are curriculum development activities involving the transfer of education/training know-how on a trans-European basis, which encompass review, overhaul and restructuring of complete (or large parts of) curricula (inter alia in order to introduce a European dimension), large-scale development of teaching material, including adaptation to the needs of the Central/Eastern European institutions and the development of multi-media education/training packages. Contemplated are continuing education and retraining schemes for higher education teachers and other trainers in priority subject areas, and for secondary education teachers undergoing higher education-level further training. They are supplemented by joint organization of short intensive courses on specialized topics in priority subject areas and language courses.

An open and distance learning provision has been designed in the eligible countries to enable students and employees to benefit from teaching programmes developed in the E.C., supplemented, where fitting, by local tuition provision. New or restructured existing higher education centers or institutions, where appropriate, are created to cater for particular education/training needs of eligible countries.

Facilities such as university libraries, teaching laboratories, teacher centers, documentation centers are to be upgraded. The universities' capacities for cooperating with industry are consummated through technology transfer units, education/training and consultancy advice to enterprises through small business centers, language centers, etc.

As to practical specific actions—education/training capacities at higher education level in priority areas, e.g. language and area studies relating to the European Community and the eligible countries respectively are increased by developing teaching materials and through exchange of training/retraining programs. And new teaching and training posts in priority areas, e.g. in the field of European Studies, at universities in eligible countries are to be established. Under the category—mobility grants for staff and students, we find that all mobility grants are in principle for the support of mobility in both directions between eligible countries on the one hand and the E.C. on the other. However, it is anticipated that flows in each direction may differ substantially interms of numbers involved and categories of participants. There is no requirement for reciprocity. In this category, teaching and training assignments are carried out at the host organization for varying periods from one week to one academic year. Priority is given to the priority subject area.

Placements abroad are undertaken by university teachers (including language teachers) or administrators for varying periods of 1 to 6 months, and visit grants are awarded for one week to one month. Grants are made to first degree level students undertaking study abroad (usually not for the first year of study) and to postgraduates undertaking further study (doctoral, teachers and even employees from eligible organizations).

In the case of students who have not yet finished their studies at their home university, precedence is given to applicants for whom the study abroad is recognized towards their home degree; special attention is given to those who intend to become teachers in a priority subject area of where otherwise there will be a multiplier effect. For applicants from E.C. countries in which attention is given where eligible countries offer interesting study possibilities outside the priority subject area, grants will be awarded for a study period at a higher education institution of normally between three months to one academic year or for longer periods to students seeking a further qualification in an E.C. member state.

Under the rubric of complementary activities grants are given to association or consortia of universities. Support will also be awarded to associations of students; teachers or administrators provided they are endorsed by the universities concerned.

Support can be provided to organizations or individuals for publications and other information activities of particular importance for the overall objectives of TEMPUS. The support will be given primarily for the preparation of a specific publication or carrying out of a specific project offering a special interest in the light of the development of the TEMPUS scheme and will always be limited in time from the outset.

Support can be given to organizations or individuals representing such organizations for surveys and studies of the development of the higher education/ training systems in eligible countries and their interaction with the E.C. and other Western countries.

Grants are awarded in youth exchange activities for short preparatory visits (up to two weeks) for the purpose of: learning about the structures in the host country/countries, establishing contacts with potential exchange partners, and participating in "mixed" workshops on the development of compatible organizational schemes and exchange models.

Of course, there are older E.C. programs that are complementary to TEMPUS, such as ERASMUS which promotes student mobility and cooperation in higher education within the E.C., and COMMETT which develops transnational training schemes in order to ensure the industrial and technological development of a unified Europe, and LINGUA which assists member states with the qualitative and quantitative improvement of foreign language teaching and training, by providing grants in support of mobility schemes and innovative projects in all sectors of education and training.

In addition, YOUTH FOR EUROPE aids young Europeans in meeting together, becoming involved in Europe by running a joint project, discovering the twelve member states of the Community, and in finding out what it is really like to live in each other's countries.

The YOUNG WORKERS' EXCHANGE PROGRAMME gives young workers (18–28) the experience of living and working conditions in another member state so that they develop skills which they need for adult and working life, including how to relate to individuals from different cultural backgrounds, and they discover shared interests with other young people from other member states, which helps to develop an awareness of a common European identity (TEMPUS, 1990).

It is possible to anticipate minor difficulties arising in the TEMPUS program akin to problems resulting in the current relationship between the universities in Western Germany with three in Eastern Germany, a case in point being interaction between the Free University and Humboldt University in Berlin. Response from the West appears to be absorption and domination more than influence and help. After the Marxist catechismical and ideological departments were eliminated within the formerly Communist state universities, the Western universities seem to insist on the adoption of their own lecturing and research structure, procedure and methodology with respect mainly to the social sciences but also to the humanities and natural sciences.

These relationships have been sorted out in Germany, but I suggest that aspects of these difficulties will be visible in the short run with the assumption of superiority by E.C. universities to those in Central/East Europe affecting temporarily the operations of TEMPUS.

Chapter Fourteen

Scandinavian Universities

Henry Wasser

Universities in Scandinavia, like political systems, have much in common as to objectives and operations. Yet emphases vary from country to country. With Norway the difference may relate to regional colleges, in Sweden bureaucratization and radical reform toward vocationalism, with Denmark local control and in Finland a binary distinction between old and new universities.

It is possible to generalize similarities. It is often asserted that Nordic countries emphasize comprehensive participation in cultural and educational activities beyond the customary broad surface involvement of most nations. They believe that such activities cannot be judged solely in terms of a single measure of quality as defined by an elite.

Sweden and Finland are traditionally somewhat more centralized than Norway in handling educational activities while Denmark leaves more responsibility to the local authorities. While there are direct links in higher education between the ministry and individual universities, for other higher education—regional and post-secondary colleges—the relationship in mainly to country-based coordinating bodies.

Extensive research programs other than basic, pure research at universities include experiments at grassroots level and "action" research projects with research and practitioners collaborating at the same level.

Nordic countries having many middle-sized towns with a declining economy create economic recovery and expansion through exceptionally strong efforts in the fields of education and culture bringing about improved social ecology, collaborative spirit and economic creativity of the locality.

In addition, the union of local culture and international orientation and involvement with problems relating to developing countries has its strongest supporters in the smaller local units in the Nordic countries.

As one veteran observer has written, the traditional power game in Scandinavia is between the central and local authorities (Eide 1986).

And, of course, there is the noted use of consensual procedure wherein Nordic countries make extensive use of "Royal Commissions." These bodies represent a wide range of interests, appointed by the government to investigate a certain field of policy and to suggest directions for further political action. Their reports are subject to broad consultations with all interested parties, after which the government presents its policy decisions to parliament, often in the form of an action program for the government.

There are, to be sure, certain differences among Scandinavian nations with respect to commitment to research and higher education: Sweden leads the way. Its percentage, for example, of Gross Domestic Product devoted to research is at present nearly 3 % and was more than 3 % by 1992. Already the highest in Europe, Sweden's Scandinavian neighbors' score is 1.6 % for Norway, 1.5 % for Finland and 1.3 % for Denmark.

Sweden, moreover, is replacing student awards with post-graduate research university posts. More than a quarter of Swedish research takes place in universities, and the increase over the next three years will be almost 200 million dollars. Basic research accounts for almost 70 % of the new money. Research funding has been extended to regional colleges, a controversial step in both Sweden and Norway since these colleges were to be primarily for teaching the disciplines. Eleven per cent of the new money is to be devoted to international collaborations, particularly with Eastern Europe.

While stressing environmental research, the initiative has brought more money to the Humanities and Social Sciences. Indeed, the Scandinavian countries as a whole seem to realize the importance of such subsidy to bringing natural science into proper perspective, in contrast to U.S.A. All of these developments are to strengthen research in these small nations so dependent on the "cutting edge" or "state of the art" research (Allardt. 1989).

Changes in these nations expectedly exposed the defects of virtues or the negatives of the positive gains. For example, reforms in Swedish higher education in the last twenty-five years are thought to be more impressive than those in other countries. Their principal goals—achievement of greater equality, creation of better linkages between education and work and an increase in participation and co-determination—were on the whole achieved. But over time defects were detected—increased bureaucratization such as applying process suitable, for support staff to faculty in department units and simply changing some features of the curriculum to transform university training into vocationally oriented training.

In Norway, the 1980's had seen lowered university prestige because increased emphasis on higher education as directly relevant to societal needs and economic growth made other post-secondary institutions more interesting for students than the universities. However, increased unemployment and closer coordination among the four universities have increased university enrollment. Conflicts remain between regional colleges and the rest of the non-university, post-secondary system, between regional colleges and the universities and between the center (Oslo) and the periphery. Universities and regional colleges compete for the same resources since regional colleges do not accept being subordinate to universities. Indeed, strengthening the universities begun in the 90's is likely to be in conflict with geographical decentralization, which has strong political support in Norway. Another cloud on the horizon is creeping managerialism replacing collegial management, perhaps more apparent at present in Norway than in the other Scandinavian countries.

Still, there is no clear hierarchy in Norwegian higher education. The nation's policy aims at equality in academic standards. Curricula and standards are harmonized in all post-secondary institutions with national standards in all teacher-training colleges.

Interest in business has led to successful private institutions at the M.B.A. level, which are subsidized by the government—a break from previous practice.

Denmark moved toward centralization in contrast to stated policy in Sweden and actual practice in Norway. Founding the Danish Research Academy and the operation of the Research Planning Council, for example, served to weaken the autonomy of the traditional system of decentralized policy in relation to allocation of research grants in institutions of higher education. Financing became more centralized. "Productivity improvement" was determined centrally in that institutions financed earlier in relation to the number of study places now allocated funding per student per unit of completed final examinations. The Ministry of Education continues to push for managerialism that is often in conflict with previous participatory democratic structures.

The new managerialism also relates to the market-driven university. In Scandinavia, regional expansion of new universities came to an end in the 1980's. Now continuing education is often the driving force of higher education policy and in Finland has particularly strong links and attachment to market forces.

While no new regional colleges have been established in Norway in recent years, the goals of those already in operation have been generally accepted by the populace. The primary aims are alternative education (short-cycle, vocationally oriented and interdisciplinary), beginning university education, and relevance to the needs of the region and recurrent education. Secondary objectives are qualification for further studies, general education, research and pedagogical reforms.

The regional colleges were expected to stimulate social, cultural and political life in the regions and thus function as a counterweight to the great urban centers. Through participation and involvement in local community life, the colleges are able to constitute an important factor of innovation. Thus Parliament in the 1980's emphasized the role of research in areas of particular relevance to the districts. Another benefit of regional colleges was supposed to be economic side-effects in the respective regions—new jobs created since the subjects taught would be relevant to local social and economic conditions e.g. fishery economics in colleges situated in fishery districts. Regional relevant study programs were expected also to stop the "brain drain" from the districts.

Typical examples of regional college programs not taught at universities or other tertiary education institutions are transportation, tourism, cultural administration, small business management, shipping and business administration, language studies for translators and interpreters, religion and parish work, and environmental protection and administration of natural resources.

But research could and did take place at regional colleges since in recruitment of regional college teachers traditional scholarly/academic criteria were the main basis for selection, working conditions were not very different from those at the universities (6–8 hours per week) and parliament was sympathetic to allocating them research funds.

Finland in its expansion of higher education established new universities especially in the northern and eastern regions, which gave birth to university towns. The trends inside these institutions have been scientific and scholarly differentiation and a consequent birth of new disciplines and chairs, for example social sciences as an independent inter-disciplinary field which grew out of increased recruitment of professionals into public service as planners and administrators and the expansion of higher education into fields earlier covered by secondary vocational education such as translation studies, the industrial arts and theater studies. Finnish universities also established supplementary education centers to retrain unemployed graduates, which acted as buffers between traditional and new forms of activity and as indicators of the distinct nature of new functions (perhaps unique to Finland as function of a university). This decentralization has also had important economic effects— increased tax revenues locally, significant consumption of services and goods from university staff and students. It has been estimated that a university with 500 employees creates another 225 jobs locally.

Regional universities also used curricular, programmatic and pedagogic experiments. Aalborg in Denmark for example was the first in Scandinavia to teach engineering with other disciplines and with a basic introductory course in technology and science, followed with upper division project oriented courses instead of a set curriculum of specified courses. Different institutes have been allowed to work out different structures suited to their own disciplinary needs and the temperament of their members.

However, at Roskilde in Denmark, while there has been acceptance of student, faculty, and staff in governing boards of study, the national government bodies interfere more in the affairs of the universities with a five-member external rectorate board in Copenhagen in control. The original experimental organization of Roskilde has been altered. The three inter-disciplinary faculties—natural sciences, humanities, and social sciences with a project-oriented two-year basic course—have been replaced by nine institutes representing traditional academic disciplines and a compressed inter-disciplinary component of the basic course into one year. The distinctiveness of the institution has thus diminished.

Sweden, however, continues to practice by far the most open decision-making process in higher education. Very little planning is done in secret and very few complaints are heard to the effect that policy positions are not declared or that information is withheld from interest groups. Swedish openness is due to tradition and to formal legislation that makes authorities prove the necessity for secrecy. For example, the famous consultative document in 1977, "Higher Education in the 1990's," was sent to at least 200 interested parties for comments. In contrast, most recent change in Norway of smaller governing senates, diminution of power of faculty deans, and closer coordination of the four universities (1988) was the result, according to many faculty, of closed door central-government planning.

Differences are also matched by influence. For example, Norwegian initiative in having the introductory course of the Examen Philosophicum compulsory for all university students is being explored by Sweden as an introductory course to higher studies comprising mainly the history and theory of science and research. A trial introductory semester course emphasizing history and theory of science is being offered at the University of Lund.

Kjell Eide, "Integrating Educational and Cultural Planning—A Synthesis of Experiences in the Nordic Countries," *UNESCO Report* 1986.

Erik Allardt, "Trends in the Promotion of Science," *Perspectives of Scientific and Technology Development*, Academy of Finland, 1989.

Chapter Fifteen

Reform in Norwegian Higher Education: The District College

Henry Wasser

The time has come to assess the reform of higher education that swept Western Europe beginning in the late 60's, coming to fruition in the 70's and presently facing, at the least, modification and, at the most, elimination. Several studies are under way. While Norway was not in the forefront of decisive reforms in the way that Sweden was, it will be contended that the changes that did occur in Norway are among the more lasting.

For many in the Norwegian academic community significant alteration of higher education structure and mission took the forms of increasing democratization in decision-making and of establishing district colleges (short-cycle higher education). Only the latter, it seems to this observer, has the importance of the new and of the durable.

According to the administrative head of the Ministry of Education of a total of 82,000 students in higher education, 42,000 come under the new definition of higher education, which comprises such specialized høgskola as music colleges of education, maritime, agricultural, engineering technology units and includes the district colleges. The remaining 40,000 are enrolled in the four universities of Oslo, Bergen, Trondheim and Tromso.

Part of the initial reform concerned the development of regional colleges or regional boards governing non-university higher education units in a region or country, including any district college located in that country. The terms "district" and "region" have been used inter-changeably but in actuality a regional board serves to administer and a regional college may be any non-university higher education unit. There are 140 of these post-secondary høgskola institutions located in 17 regions. A regional board (Det Regionale Høgskolestyret) may exist where there is no district college as in the region of Hordaland (the Bergen area). This governing board has nine members, five of whom are selected by the politicians of the ruling political party, via the ministry, two by college faculty and two by college students.

The Hordaland regional board director asserts that many regions are discussing removal of student and faculty staff representatives with only political appointees left. He predicts this modification of democratic reform will occur in two or four years. He concedes that this predicted move runs counter to the one that changed appointment by the education minister of the rector of Bergen College of Education (his former position) to election by the college senate.

For selection of staff, district college criteria were similar to those for the university except that experience was weighted more. In the early 70's district college staff, in the opinion of several observers, were better qualified than their peers at the university because of the attraction of the novel, experimental, imaginative curricula and faculty in the district colleges. Moreover, in the period of 1965–1972 many of the more imaginative and independent students were to be found in the district and regional colleges.

The faculty, however, for the most part, continue to cling to a university orientation since their professional work will be honored by university professors to whom they look for such esteem. An anomaly was that the shift away from university pure research toward practical local applied research has increased despite the political change to a conservative government more responsive to university needs.

The most radical district college was Upland located in Lilliehammer. It emphasized psychology, the individual, and was consciously opposed to a highly competitive educational system such as it detected in the U.S.A. Like Roskilde University Center, the college's programs were problem-oriented. The process was to define a problem of a practical nature, sort out a particular difficulty, refine it, and gather information from books and studies in the field that related to the solution of the problem. The objective was not simply to seek a direct answer developed from a book but to look for individual evaluations of the problem.

Cooperative orientation was another key motto wherein students worked in groups without a teacher-student authority relationship. Teachers acted mainly as tutors (8–10 students per teacher, the number determined in part by available room space and number of staff).

Group exams were given where the students in the group defined their own problems for the exam. They prepared 3 or 4 themes for an exam. There were 3–5 per exam group with 10–14 days to prepare a paper. After a pass / fail evaluation, the group met with the assessment trio, 2 insiders and 1 outsider, for a more precise evaluation.

When the system was first established, students would either pass or fail. Later the group was differentiated so that one or more of the group could pass or fail.

Despite a more conservative atmosphere in the country, group work orientation remains, group exams remain, all courses now require an individual essay, and the individual student is emphasized more.

Regional and district colleges differ from each other in workload from as few as 4 to as many as 14–18 hours per week. The Telemark district college at Bø has 8 hours per week for its lecturers. In the universities lecturers reach 6 hours and professors 4 hours per week. Courses in district colleges generally are in business and social sciences with natural sciences and mathematics at a minimum and humanities rare. While Upland follows this typical course pattern, Telemark District College at Bø has a *grunnfag* (one-year course) in English. The ministry's officer for district colleges believes history, English and French *grunnfags* will be added to many district colleges since so many of the faculty are sufficiently trained to teach such.

Upland's approach was cross-disciplinary, and it recruited staff of differing backgrounds. It was difficult apparently for the staff to work in inter-disciplinary fashion. Subsequently, the faculty became more discipline-oriented and it was left to the student to be inter- or cross-disciplinary. The staff was not given the opportunity to be trained toward inter-disciplinarity since they were recruited just 3 months before teaching, insufficient time for orientation. Nevertheless, Upland was able to avoid Roskilde's problems by establishing a course catalogue and formulating precise frames within which the student would work. While at Roskilde the student wrote his own ticket within a discipline e.g. a physics student could go anywhere, at Upland there were 3–5 areas to work with and the students could define their own studies within one of the problem areas.

The average age of the students was 24–25; up to 25 % of the students were enrolled without the ordinary exam. Their ranks included shop stewards from industry, students from technical upper level schools, fishermen, farmers, newspaper / media personnel with dubious preparation but with good positions in radio / television / press, which mixed theory and practice. Upland did not succeed so well with young students because the social set-up of the district college was a shock, too different for them. Other regional colleges did take mainly young school learners.

Despite university anxiety and the short-cycle nature of programs, considerable research did go on at various regional colleges. Indeed, so many were on leave for research that the full-time teaching staff was often depleted, forcing reliance on part-time temporaries, according to a former district college rector. There has been strong local support for research since local authorities receive from district colleges a lot of research data and analyses for their own decision-making. Even change in government from social-democratic to conservative will not affect this local self-interest. But local enthusiasm is for applied research. A celebrated case displayed local politicians' anger over a district college faculty member receiving a grant for research in a West African dialect, not of cost / benefit value for the local county authorities.

Since they were founded, the desirable size of district colleges has been discussed. It is conceded that the newer colleges are too small—several under 1,000 students in the sparsely settled regions. Although the Ottosen committee had suggested 20 district colleges, one for each of Norway's regions and a maximum size of 4,000 students, at present fifteen years later it is believed that Norway should be limited to its present 17 colleges, each of which would be considered viable with an enrollment of 1,000 to 1,500.

The age-cohort population is predicted to increase for the next 7–8 years, perhaps 8 % in total. The universities are to remain the same size; indeed a number of politicians argue that the University of Oslo at 19,000 and the University of Bergen at 15,000 are too large and propose to cut their student enrollment. The increase, therefore, would be accommodated mainly in the district colleges and other høgskola. A contemplated 25 % cut in teach training will also add to regional college enrollment.

Ranks and salary for faculty at the district colleges and other høgskola are the same as at the universities except that the rank of professor does not exist. The highest rank is docent, roughly equivalent to British reader and is considered a senior title. There are about 22 such positions in the district college system.

The universities concede that the district colleges are here to stay. In spite of initial doubts, they do not now believe that research allotment to district interferes with their own research money allocation in that contract research with different agencies of government is the district college mainstay for research funds. Universities would grant an increasing role in technology expansion to these new institutions. They seem content with responding to enrollment demand by allocating under 10% of the entering class to those without an *Artium*, admitted on work experience, age, etc.

While universities disagree with høgskola assertions that external examiners guarantee uniform standards, which, they say, worked only when there was one university, they concede the advantage to higher education that comes with the consequent contact between høgskola and university faculty.

University officials worry that district colleges are partly responsible for taking away or cutting down university offerings e.g. the first course in German is given at 13 different institutions, mostly non-university høgskola.

Consequently, the German program at the University of Bergen has been sharply reduced. They would like to think of district colleges not as supplement to, substitute for, or even preparatory for, universities, but rather as alternatives to the university reacting to social needs to which the university cannot or will not respond.

Judging district colleges a success is acceptable on several grounds. The quality of the staff even according to university standards has been established. Students often select a district college not as a second choice, but as a first choice because of geographical proximity and the attraction of innovative teaching and practical programs. The existence of district colleges, especially the more experimental ones like Upland, has influenced rigidly traditional universities to be more flexible in their curricula. Social need and political pressure will insure that the expansion of age-cohort in the next 18 years will benefit the enrollment of district colleges.

Sweden without much success attempted to enact decentralization centrally but Norway has never had that kind of power at the center. Local, grass-root political strength has always been impressive, and it would seem that district colleges are a logical outcome of that localization. They have become the cultural counter-weight that regionalists have felt they needed in dealing with the force of national universities, which in turn appear to have accommodated with some reluctance to their existence and influence.

Chapter Sixteen

The Idea of Contemporary Europe

Henry Wasser

Those interested in the idea of Europe as an identity often try to trace the origin of the concept or the word. Usually one decides that Europe means nothing until the development of medieval Christianity, that one can use the term Europe upon reaching the period of Charlemagne. Obviously this had a certain useful meaning when Latin was a common language. Now in a sense there is no common language in Europe, although I suppose we have an international language for certain places in the world, i.e. English. So, the development of Christianity appears to lead to the use, the "old" use of the term Europe. Certainly there are scholars, other than those committed to the Common Market, who believe this. An excellent periodical exists, formerly *The History of European Ideas* now *The European Legacy* whose editor-in-chief is an Israeli professor of philosophy at Haifa University, a circumstance that reminds us of the co-optation of Israel within a European dimension. Those who go to conferences dealing with Europe often find scholars from non-European countries. This may have to do with the European origin of many scholars, and Israel is a part of that.

Obviously nationalism is a great factor in any possible integration; it, in a sense, has never been overcome, but in some fashion for the sake of European unity, nationalism has to be superseded. Europe has an identity for the future. One spoke of Europe as a oneness in the past, then of intervening developments. Then what is Europe as a future? My guess is that Europe and the sense of Europe as an identity in the future has come about in the following way: First there was movement towards cooperation on matters of education, then there was a stoppage and then more recently again there was a coming together. Why? Because of the challenge of high technology. So the economic imperative of the change toward high technology may conduce towards European identity. What do I mean? It is simply that high technology demands enormous capital, enormous resources that only Europe as Europe can provide. Only the superpowers, United States, Soviet Union, possibly Japan, and perhaps China some day can provide that and the only way that Europe can respond to the challenge of high technology is to operate as an integrated Europe. Those economic challenges may bring about an identity or unity of Europe which neither exhortatory language nor cultural identification can produce. The oneness of Europe in the future will come about from the economic imperative. One notices a recent conference in Paris, which was a European response to high technology with people from various countries in the Common Market, industrialists, professors from universities, meeting on the particular topic. There is, of course, an older view of Europe as cultural identity of European inhabitants as stated by Denis de Rougement who was the "grand old man" of this approach. He said that the Europe to be united is a way of life, of experiencing the world and of perceiving human relationships—thus a culture in the broadest sense of the term. There are, of course, other organizations that work toward this. There is the European Cultural Foundation that cooperates with O.E.C.D., with the Council of Europe, with the U.N., with the E.E.C. It is a foundation, well-financed by the lotteries of the Netherlands, which has established institutes in various countries on environment, media, education, social policy, strategic studies and the like. There is one in Belgium, one in Paris, one in Germany, one in the Netherlands, one in England. They always work towards a European identity. The European Cultural Foundation has recently established an Institute for studying the media, television in various European countries. While there is a general movement in that direction, it is the "economic imperative" again—electronic advance, etc.—that will be the prime motor. Much as I would like to think that philosophic and cultural imperatives would bring European identity, they help, but it is the economic imperative even more than the political imperative that will accomplish such.

Jacques Lang attempts to define European identity by criticizing Americanization. Lang's is an odd, if somewhat serious statement because in his sharp critique of American culture he speaks from a sense of European culture as if American culture were antagonistic to it. That leads to a second point, which I find fascinating, that is, in the words of Milan Kundera, the Czech novelist, the disappearance of middle-central Europe. He writes of the events of '68 when the Soviet Union crushed the Czech "spring." What they thought they were doing, the intellectuals, the cultural leaders of Czechoslovakia, was fighting for Europe, not especially for Czechoslovakia but for the survival or Europe and European culture, that's what they thought they were fighting against the Soviet Union for. Physically they could not do that, but did in other ways. Then Kundera says when it came to that Europe they were fighting to save, it no longer existed; instead he finds in France and elsewhere "Americanization." European culture understood in central European terms no longer exists because of the Americanization of Western Europe.

The third point is this. There could be a deeper kind of European culture, a stronger sense of European identity within the university and educated circles that intellectuals, now in a fallow period, might develop out of this deeper concern. The next step would be to revitalize in the way they revitalized some decades ago. But the vitalization and intellectuality and intellectuals might come from the deeper sense of European identity if it exists. The fourth thing I am reminded of is that one may get another sense of identity, if not universal, perhaps possible for Europe is the culture of science. I mean scientists always seem, at least in recent decades, less provincial than the rest of us because the terminology, the concepts science deals with know no boundaries. And it is possible that this too will add meaning to a concept of Europe. If one develops a sense of the culture of science to meet the challenge of technology and to meet the challenge of the scientific development of the great powers, that would create a European identity After all, the largest atom smasher in the world is in Europe; there are numerous developments in research on nuclear matters, physics and the like which lead persuasively to an identity of Europe. Again perhaps there is an economic imperative in these enormous advances of science. There again no individual European country can accomplish such advances by itself. What the U.S. can do by itself, what the Soviet Union can do by itself can only be done in Europe by all of Europe because of the enormous expenditure of capital required. Only by pooling resources can Europe match the science of the continental nations, this then is another factor that may conduce to European identity.

One may think of the development in America, in the United States of America as possibly the raw model for what might be led to, for Europe. There is, to be sure, the history of the United States, which shows an increasing homogenization. For example, once language was the same but the regional accents were sharply different. One does not find much in the way of regional accents any more. And that is probably the result of radio and television. United States is a vast continental nation and over time has a greater sense of itself as a nation. But there are many other kinds of differences than accent. I do not find a greater awareness of Europe in U.S.A. that previously existed. We still have great difficulties with language studies in American universities. They have not flourished in the way they might. Then, of course, so far as Europe is concerned, there is the great counterweight in that the whole West of U.S.A. leans towards the Pacific and Asian countries. That region does not have nearly the awareness of Europe found east of the Mississippi

Rivers. And in terms of curriculum, program, we do not find nearly so much awareness of Europe as one would expect, given the European origin of many migrants of previous generations.

The great Greek poet Cavafy, writing about Alexandria where the conflicts among the Hebrews, the native Egyptians, and the Christians—we may recall that it was the Christians who destroyed the magnificent library of Alexandria—the various peoples in Alexandria amidst their conflicts would be unified only when there was an enemy at the gates and in a superb poem Cavafy describes that. So I suppose what I am saying is that contrary to the assertions by Schopenhauer and others the positive exhortation in words is not likely to bring about the unification of Europe but rather the external challenges will bring it about. When you have superpowers that in any second can blow up the world, you have an enormous external challenge for unification of response. When you have tremendous economic problems in Latin America, in Africa, in developing nations everywhere, that situation can bring about a unified response, a common response, and a response of the Common Market to those very problems. So we may become optimistic about the unity of Europe. As to the Common Market, external challenges can bring about unity.

I think that if one speaks of Eurocentric, one has to speak, when the U.S.A. deals with things, of U.S.A.-centric and I believe that even in such matters as NATO, United States tends to be U.S.A.-centric despite the collectivity of NATO. It tends to deal with individual nations in slightly different manners. It may deal in NATO terms with Germany in one sense and with Norway in a slightly different sense. One has to keep in mind the same thing in connection with the Third World. We tend to think of everything in East-West terms and yet there are certain regions where we think we decide and that are important to us and there are certain other regions that do not quite have that importance for us. We are inclined to think in East-West terms and where it does not have that importance to us, we may be more permissive and more responsive. In matters of collectivity or unity the way U.S.A. deals with things is not particularly conducive to this kind of unification and once again I go back to a point that it is not wise usually to look in terms of unifications to the U.S.A. as a role model.

The position and relation of the United States and the view in the United States of a unified Europe evolves and changes depending upon changes of administration in Washington, it evolves with the change of relationship with the Soviet Union, it evolves with the change of sense of what economic powers or the like may be in Europe. What I am saying is that I do not think there has ever been one consistent view of unified Europe in the United States; it has changed according to these variables. The second question I want to articulate: what does it mean that Gonzales out of power in Spain can oppose its entrance into NATO and once in power can switch around so sharply that the referendum to enter NATO is won by two million votes. I do not know what it means, in the customary sense of meaning when a politician out of power does a 180-degree turn when in power. Does it refer internally? Does it mean changed polling data or opinion until Spain entered the Common Market? And now it counterbalances this, if you will, in terms of its membership in E.E.C. The second question commences with my noting that in the elections to the European Parliament, which may follow, close upon or just before member states' national elections, the results are rather different. Now, are the results different because the elections to the European Parliament are the results of what the soul says? Or the mind really wants? But national member state elections have to do more with self-interest, is that the reason for the discrepancy? Will an increasing awareness of a European parliament lend to a more focused idea of Europe?